DESIGNING GENIUS

Praise for Designing Genius

As a heart officer, what I know to be true is when you focus on people, everything grows for good. Amilya and Designing Genius guides leaders to serving with greater impact with longer term results.

– **Claude Silver, Chief Heart Officer at VaynerMedia**

As business leaders, everything we do has a purpose. The goal is to be successful, but how do we get there? Amilya's book is the perfect "how-to" for the world we live in. She gives readers the tools to be more intentional and let our actions guide us to achieve more impactful outcomes. Get out of your own way, buy the book, and get started on the road to success!

– **Jeffrey Hayzlett, primetime TV and podcast host, speaker, author, and part-time cowboy**

Amilya's commitment to serving people to the fullest is demonstrated yet again in her latest book Designing Genius. This book will bring tremendous value to anyone looking to be more intentional in designing their business or life.

– **David Meltzer, co-founder of Sports 1 Marketing**

There's never been a better time than now to rethink what we want for our life. Designing Genius is the perfect guide to take the reader from self-discovery to action to designing a life that is joyful, productive, thriving, and successful.

– **Mark Goulston, author of *Just Listen***

What we think is what we become. This book is the first step to creating a life that most could only dream of.

> – Greg S. Reid, American author, speaker, filmmaker

More than ever, people want to live a life built on what matters most to them. Designing Genius teaches you how to design your life with intention—year after year. Reach for this book to create clarity, set your focus, and chart your course to fulfillment, happiness, and balance—personally and professionally.

> – **Luke Iorio, host of the On This Walk podcast, former CEO and president of the Institute for Professional Excellence in Coaching (iPEC)**

After reading Designing Genius, it is easy to see why companies are utilizing it to fix their "people problems." As a CEO who has spent over 20 years in global business consulting and crisis management, I can honestly say that the more leaders understand human behavior, the less crisis they create.

> – **Stephynie Malik, CEO and crisis expert at SMALIK Enterprises**

Amilya Antonetti has mastered the science of human behavior and seeks to empower every person she encounters. After experiencing a grave and life-altering tragedy, Amilya helped me to regain a positive mindset. She also devised a structured plan to optimize my goals. She's a genius (no pun intended), and I'm honored to know her.

> – **Dr. Rolanda Schmidt, CEO, management and ministry expert**

Praise for Designing Genius

Designing Genius is a great reminder that people are a company's greatest asset. This book shows that focusing on the people around you and being the best you possible is key to creating unity within the workplace.

– **Dan Macuga, chief communications and marketing officer at USNA**

Amilya's commitment to serving people and designing healthier places to work and to create is an example all leaders can learn from.

– **Michael Nouri, screen and stage actor**

Designing Genius provides the behavior modification tools to bring your life and business to the next level. Give yourself the gift of this book and come back to it as often as you can.

– **Renée Marino, speaker, author, communication coach**

Amilya cuts through the noise and addresses the choices we make and the behaviors that drive our lives. Her insights and tools provide solutions that yield rapid results. Implementing what I learned from her has helped me grow personally and professionally, and this book will help you do the same.

– **Susie Miller, leadership and communication expert**

Your brain has such power. Most of us underuse its power and often harm ourselves or others. Designing Genius is the guide you need to help realign your brain for maximum results in your life and profession.

– **Ramon Ray, publisher of zoneofgenius.com**

DESIGNING GENIUS

Success Is an INWARD Journey

AMILYA ANTONETTI
with
PATRICIA WOOSTER

Designing Genius: Success Is an Inward Journey

Copyright 2022 © Amilya Antonetti & Patricia Wooster

All information, techniques, ideas and concepts contained within this publication are of the nature of general comment only and are not in any way recommended as individual advice. The intent is to offer a variety of information to provide a wider range of choices now and in the future, recognizing that we all have widely diverse circumstances and viewpoints. Should any reader choose to make use of the information contained herein, this is their decision, and the contributors (and their companies), authors and publishers do not assume any responsibilities whatsoever under any condition or circumstances. It is recommended that the reader obtain their own independent advice.

WosterMedia LLC
Tampa, Florida
woostermediabooks.com

Hardback ISBN: 979-8-9861607-3-3
Paperback ISBN: 979-8-9861607-4-0

Designing Genius: Success Is an Inward Journey is under copyright protection. No part of this book may be used or reproduced in any manner whatsoever without written permission except in the case of brief quotations embodied in critical articles and reviews. Printed in the United States of America. All rights reserved.

The moral right of Amilya Antonetti & Patricia Wooster as the author of this work has been asserted by her in accordance with the Copyrights, Designs and Patents Act of 1988.

Published by WoosterMedia LLC
woostermediabooks.com

Table of Contents

Free Bonus .... *x*
Foreword .... *xi*
Introduction *1*

Chapter 1: What If Everything You Learned
　　　　　about Living Your Best Life Was Wrong? 7

Chapter 2: A Game with No Rules 25

Chapter 3: What Is Designing Genius? 41

Chapter 4: It Starts with One Word 55

Chapter 5: Focusing on the Journey 71

Chapter 6: Your Key Ingredients 85

Chapter 7: Rules of the Game 101

Chapter 8: Rule Starters 117

Chapter 9: Living the Perfect Day 137

Chapter 10: Genius Living 153

In Gratitude *161*
About the Authors *163*
Additional Free Bonus *167*
Thank You *169*

Free Bonus

Start Designing Genius Today!

Want to jumpstart your journey toward living your highest and best life?

Check out the free Designing Genius Toolbox that comes with this book. In this toolbox you will receive:

- Tools and games to play with your family
- #1 Strategy to make any of your goals a reality
- $50 Coupon for the Designing Genius course

Scan the QR code below to download your Toolbox, so you can start living your life by design today.

Foreword

What is happiness, and what can we do to achieve it?

The "pursuit of happiness," aside from being a key aspect of the U.S. Declaration of Independence, is baked into humankind's very essence. Despite our individual differences, the desire for happiness is inherent in each of us—it's a core part of our human nature.

Internet definitions describe happiness as "the mental feeling of well-being" or "an emotional state characterized by feelings of joy, satisfaction, contentment, and fulfillment."

In my own personal lexicon, I like to take these excellent definitions a step deeper. For me, "happiness" is defined as "a genuine and ongoing feeling of joy and peace of mind; the result of living congruently with one's values."

In other words, it's only when our behaviors are in alignment with our values that we can truly be sustainably happy. And this understanding, I believe, is key to reaching the end goal in our pursuit.

Some will argue that it's best not to "pursue" happiness but rather to let it come to you.

The very nature of that well-intended advice, however, leaves us floating aimlessly like the feather in the movie *Forrest Gump*, directed only by uncontrollable gusts of wind. Luck—and happiness—*can* happen, and that feather (or you) *may* eventually end up in a good place. But…probably not.

Instead, I believe that we need to take control of those behaviors that are most likely to take us to our intended destination.

Of course, there's a lot we cannot control. But there's also plenty that we can. That's where our choices become important.

We can control what happiness means to us personally.

We can control what our highest values are.

We can also control our thoughts and our actions.

This is an excellent beginning.

And as we continue working to align our behaviors with our values and "design our best life," it's helpful to have the right tools at hand.

That's where Amilya Antonetti and Patricia Wooster come in. As wise and helpful guides, they provide their readers with nothing less than a road map to attaining success and happiness.

In *Designing Genius*, the authors help individuals move from where they are now to where they want to be, instilling a sense of self-confidence as the reader journeys through a process that is both practical and enjoyable.

As hinted at earlier, it's vital that we are able to appreciate and understand the concepts of success and happiness AND that we are well-equipped as we strive to attain them.

Designing Genius is truly about just that: it's about bringing into alignment all the areas of your life that are most important…to *you!*

Follow the sage wisdom of these two wonderful role models, practitioners, and teachers, and be prepared to live at a higher level of enjoyment, peace of mind, and happiness than you may have ever considered possible.

Wishing you Stratospheric Success and Happiness,

Bob Burg
Coauthor of *The Go-Giver*

Introduction

How do you know what is actually important? I was sitting at a table in a large boardroom, surrounded by lawyers and staring at a thick contract. The words on these papers were about to change my life and the lives of thousands of my employees, vendors, and customers. I looked at the person on my right and then at the person on my left. As I slowly gazed at every other person sitting at this table, a sinking feeling pulled deep within me. At that moment, I realized I didn't like any of these people.

I know this sounds harsh, but in a flash, I became "aware" that the people gathered around the table were the people I had been pouring myself into day after day. The best of my time, energy, and attention was given to each of them. Every one of these people and their problems are what filled my mind and pulled my focus to their wants and needs, even when I returned home at night. Yet as I looked around the room, getting ready to make one of the biggest decisions of my life, I could feel that NONE of them cared about me—the person—at all!

They cared about what I could do for them, but they knew little about me. They were good at their roles, but the passion and purpose behind why I started this company, SoapWorks, were not reflected as they anxiously stared at me sitting at the end of the table with the pen in my hand. I almost laughed out loud. Then a very clear thought floated into my consciousness: Where are the people I actually care about?

My company started as a mother's race against the clock to find the cause of a myriad of breathing and skin conditions spiraling out of control. A series of events had me fighting for my son's life as I ran from doctor to doctor, burning through cash and seeking any answer to stop my baby's relentless cries and clear the hopelessness that hung as a dark death cloud over him. What started as a quest to find a solution developed into a human- and earth-friendly company called SoapWorks. Not just "a" company, but one that ushered in the "green movement". Before my company, "green" was just a color. This company was now being purchased for a significant amount of money—millions of dollars. But at what expense?

One of the most powerful questions I have ever been asked came during one of the first times I met Oprah. She asked me, "What do you know for sure?" What I know is that everything of value comes at a cost. The question is not, "What do you want?" The question is, "What are you willing to pay or sacrifice for it?"

As I sat in that boardroom, my mind was rewinding all the nights. Instead of tucking my son and daughter into bed, I had my nose in the computer, or I was in the warehouse unloading a delivery, taking inventory, or putting together an order. I put out every fire and served every person by giving the best of me to people that never even saw me for who I am.

The people I loved the most got the leftovers, and strangers got my best. Talk about mixed-up priorities. I poured everything into my business, employees, investors, and the media. I had a big house in Arizona, an apartment in NYC, a place in California, a gorgeous partner, beautiful children, and I was able to retire my father—all the things I supposedly cared about and wanted when I was growing up. Yet there was no evidence in my life that I valued any of them. I was always busy. I had homes I had not been to in months and more holidays and vacations I missed. Let's not even talk about school and sporting events.

I was chasing all these people and things to fill a big, empty hole within me. I was looking to be accepted in all the wrong areas. I was traveling and hanging out in incredible locations, but I was alone. I was taking care of my employees and their needs, but I wasn't taking care of my own.

I knew that to change my situation and circumstances, I first had to look internally and start with me. Our minds are tightly connected to what we do first and last, so I decided to be intentional with the first twenty-two minutes of my morning. I designed these twenty-two minutes for sustainable impact and got clear on my morning *me* minutes. I refer to this as my morning H.U.G., which answers the question: What am I?

Healing –
What you do not heal will hurt others.
Understanding –
If you seek to understand "self," you can set clear intentions.
Without intention, you are guessing your way through your life.
Gratitude –
What you are not grateful for, you will lose.

From your H.U.G., you can set a clear intention with equal energy. This became my "give and get" of the day, and this was *huge* for me. By nature, I am a giver. It is easy for me to give to others, but I struggle to ask for help.

When I understood how these two energies were necessary to grow, I was able to build both sides of the energetic loop into my morning. What is your intentional "give" for the day? This is your service to others. What is your "get" for the day? This is your one "ask" for the day.

This general framework for my morning mindset started to build a foundation for me to grow and get into stronger alignment with myself. This began to develop my confidence and ushered in better accountability, so I no longer found myself so far off track that I could not recognize the girl in the mirror.

Once I worked it out for myself, I discovered that other people in my position were struggling with the same issues. They were experiencing the same push and pull for their time, energy, and focus. And while they were considered highly successful in one area of their life, they were failing in others.

I saw the magnitude of the dissatisfaction, pain, and unnecessary energy being expended in all the wrong places. As I looked around, I spotted the same patterns everywhere with parents, relationships, workplaces, and friendships.

Life, love, and business would be easy if it were not for the people.

This one phrase hurts my heart. Every single person has these triggered hurt spots—yes, if you have a pulse, you have a hurt spot. Without pulling out the root and planting a healthy relationship seed, you will repeatedly loop back to the same unhealed wound. Let's be clear—diving into Netflix and a gallon of ice cream is not going to heal the hurt either. These are momentary distractions and blockers to the pain but not deep-rooted healing.

If the fix were this simple, more people worldwide would be healed and no longer triggered by something that happened years ago. We would not be reattracting the same people, lessons, and experiences that are not good for us. Deep-rooted healing is hard, but the other side of the hurt is healing.

As a behaviorist, here is what I know for sure: people cause a lot of unintended pain. It is never the tactical learning of life that derails us. Tactics don't break our hearts, tear apart a business, infuse hateful feelings into our schools, dismantle our families, or stop people from talking to each other for so long that they can't remember why they stopped speaking in the first place. The analytical side of life is not

Introduction

what causes our spirit to spiral into regret as we near the finish line of life.

No, my friend, these things are always at the hand of people and their choices. Here is the thing: I love people. I am mesmerized by people and captivated by the hero's journey. I scream and cheer like a schoolgirl when I watch the magic born within people in simple gestures that light up someone's soul.

It seems that during horrific tragedies, and in the darkest of times, we witness the true power of people. We see the abundance of light when people unite for good. Just now, I am reflecting on so many unforgettable moments I've witnessed during tragedies like the Boston Marathon bombing, 9/11, the Vegas shooting, Hurricane Sandy, and hundreds of other world events where the stories of the kindness within people and the heroism of humans united our spirits as we watched impeccable beauty and grace.

So, what the heck is going on within people when we see the opposite? How do people get so far away from their True North or internal compass? How on earth have companies, communities, and families gotten on opposite sides of the fence? Don't we need each other?

Take a walk with me as I take the complexities of people and make "what is really happening" much simpler to understand. See, what I know for sure is that what you think is happening within you and for the person across from you, IS NOT WHAT IS ACTUALLY HAPPENING.

Crazy right? The people tools we will introduce to you will quickly reveal what is going on. We made this human behavior experience fun and impactful, so it will be easy for you to follow along and experience immediate results.

Why? Because none of us have time to waste. None of us want to spend another moment focused on the wrong people, wrong priorities, and unaligned goals. None of us want to live in pain, with regret, or by hurting others. And because we cannot teach what we do not know.

To be clear: this isn't just words on paper; it's a journey. So, get ready for genius living because we are starting with the most important person here—YOU!

– Amilya

Chapter 1

What If Everything You Learned about Living Your Best Life Was Wrong?

There's an old Zen saying: *The way you do one thing is the way you do everything.* My clients love the simplicity of that adage once they've learned how to unlock the secrets to designing their life in a way that aligns with their innate genius. It might sound too easy, but that's the beauty of human behaviorism. We identify why we do what we do, decide whether we are receiving the desired outcome, and then make changes based on that information. Human behavior and behavior modification are not therapy. They are not reliant on other people. And that puts us directly in the driver's seat with tools that work instantly.

Living a life by design, which I call "Designing Genius," does not come naturally or by accident. And it is not for lack of trying that keeps us spinning our wheels. Many of us have tried all kinds of personal development tactics that leave us trying to solve the wrong problems. We live within the noise of wanting more money, time, or happiness, which are not the real issues. How many wealthy people do you read about who are miserable? How many people do you know who have plenty of time and still can't get out of their own way?

Whether you are building a team, growing a business, amplifying a relationship, or trying to teach your kids life skills, this book is filled with quick behavior modification tools that are easy, fun, and everyone can enjoy. The concept of Designing Genius works in every stage of our lives. I have used these tools with everyone from high-achieving executives and celebrities to people struggling through life challenges. These tools work because they create a new standard for living by identifying what is most important to YOU and how to bring more of those things into your life while eliminating the distractions, thoughts, and opinions no longer serving you.

The only thing standing between you and designing your genius life is an unidentified behavior. It is easy to believe that if we had more money and time our life would be better, but you will soon discover they are a byproduct of a true alignment with your best self. It is like digging a hole with a toothpick and discovering we have no purpose for the hole. We know we put in a lot of time and effort, but all we have to show for it is exhaustion and a broken tool.

Whether we like it or not, our thoughts and actions start with us. It's not about fixing other people or changing situations beyond our control. Success of any kind is an internal game. Our lives have a past, present, and future, and within those are experiences, feelings, and emotions that lead to our behavior. This is what we dive into in this book . . . our behavior. For many of us, we have never slowed down long enough to understand why we act the way we do in certain situations. Or if what we claim to believe are really our beliefs. When was the last time you really examined your reaction to a problem? Or wondered where the judgment you feel is rooted in your life? Or why sometimes you overreact more emotionally than a situation calls for?

For most of us, the answer is *never*.

Our behavior is either protecting or defending something in our lives. Consider the person who comes off as gruff or indifferent. What could they be protecting or defending? Being hurt, let down, feeling not good enough, or receiving judgment? Maybe they think it is easier to push people away than be hurt or abandoned by others.

How about the person who posts a false narrative of their life on social media? Could they be trying to distract people from what their life is really like? Or are they protecting themselves by projecting what they really want? Avoidance behavior is alive and well in today's digital and immediate gratification world. The "perception" is that it is easier to mask what we feel than to face our struggles head-on. What we are avoiding has a significant impact on our time, money, energy, and resources. Avoidance is the joy killer that takes energy away from building a genius life.

When we understand what we are protecting or defending, we have an opportunity to understand and see who we really are and how we show up in the world. We know from behavioral studies that something is always happening in every situation, and what you think is happening is rarely what is going on. Until we begin the journey to understanding ourselves, we never understand other people. Through understanding, we gain clarity, and with clarity, we have an opportunity to choose which behavior serves us today. If we appear gruff because we have gotten hurt in the past by someone close, we can start asking ourselves better questions like, how is this behavior serving me today? Is it pushing energy away or pulling it in? Is it better to remove the risk of being hurt by acting a certain way? Or does it make more sense to choose a different behavior, so I have an opportunity for a better result?

Here is a hard truth: What was useful in the past may no longer be needed to get us what we desire tomorrow. Our behavior today will keep us rooted in today. Instead, we want our behavior to align with who we are becoming and the life we want to design. This moves us away from repeatedly doing the same things and getting the same undesired results. Throwing a tantrum, storming off, and slamming doors may have brought you the attention you wanted as a child, but today gets you ostracized and labeled as difficult. This is just one small example of how your behavior creates the gap between you and genuine connection and belonging.

The thing that we as humans need more than anything in this world is to belong. Our misaligned behavior includes walking away from conversations and leaving things unspoken and incomplete. This, among other behaviors, creates pain, hurt, and disconnection from yourself and the very people with whom you wish to connect. Your fear of facing your life is the gap that stops you from living your designed life. Now that you are older, you can choose to replace that behavior with a new one that gets the desired result.

Together we will break down this process piece by piece. This book will teach you how to intentionally modify and choose the behaviors that bring the right energy into your life. The beauty of behavior modification is that the tools work immediately to get a result. Whether you are looking to optimize your current life, solve a problem, or live with more intention, what you learn in this book will amplify what is currently working for you and eliminate what is not.

Designing a life that feels the way we want it to feel is a challenge for most of us. Much of the information that exists on how to elevate your life, advance your career, improve relationships, and find a sense of peace are lacking some significant facts. If I were to ask you to choose one of two lives where one has all the money, riches, and material abundance one could ever spend but was lonely, bitter, and resentful, or the second, where you have everything to maintain your desired lifestyle and feel seen, heard, recognized, and valued, which life would you choose?

This is why we start by asking how we want our lives to *feel*. Then we can build a strong foundation based on those feelings and layer up from there. By starting with "self", we put the strongest building blocks in place first. After that, we can add in the other pieces that represent abundance for your life.

Are You a Victim?

How refreshing is it to know that we are not a victim of anything. No matter how tragic or wonderful, our past has shaped who we are today. My difficult childhood created my resilience and my drive and led me to build my legacy around healing others' pain. Without my history, I would not be who I am today. At an early age, the behaviors I learned helped me adapt and survive a difficult and traumatic childhood.

Would I change my experience? No, because my experiences prepared me for everything that came next in my life. Like many of us who have done the impossible, we would not have had the courage to start if we had any idea of how difficult the journey would be. There is much to be said about behavior and the fact that we learn and modify as we grow. Once we have the tools to identify what behaviors have served their purpose, we gain the confidence to release them because we understand it is a natural part of our growth. Without strong self-awareness and self-evaluation, we flatline and get stuck. Nothing is meant to stay the same forever, not even our behavior. As humans, we were designed for learning, growth, and curiosity. This is all part of the human experience.

Does this mean the work is done? No. Far from it. Now, it's about keeping who we are as a person because there's nothing wrong with us. Our scars become our unique abilities. Our imperfections are the keys to unlocking the doors for growing into the best versions of ourselves. By celebrating them for the time they did serve us, we can release them when they are no longer needed. We can learn to free ourselves from our past thinking and welcome better thoughts and solutions for tomorrow. We accomplish this by removing the behaviors and activities no longer serving us. It is a choice. Today's thoughts build our tomorrow self.

Yes, we will choose to let some things go, and that's okay. And we will learn some new things that will feel weird at first, and that's okay too. A hero must do difficult things, and nothing is more difficult than taking responsibility for our life and our story. Isn't that the point of Robert Frost's poem, "The Road Not Taken"? To persevere and take the path that leads to the right destination? The initial discomfort of change is a better alternative to staying where we are, and feeling like we feel, for the next five, ten, twenty, or fifty years if we are not satisfied with our current location.

A victim, on the other hand, gets stuck. They believe everything is done "to them" instead of "for them" and hands their life over to fate. They look backward, glancing over their shoulder, and cling to their familiar behaviors. A victim has no say in how they feel and how their life unfolds. Life happens to them as they take a passive role in their life's journey.

In contrast, a survivor perseveres to live and grow from their past experiences. They take an active role in moving forward despite past hardships and pain. They choose to live a life of choice rather than die within the suffering someone else chooses for them.

We can either live within our situation or grow from our situation. So many people get hit with a hard slap from life and stay there forever. They stay in that pain. Life gets very small as a victim. The situation becomes the root of your story and your identifier. Unfortunately, there will be people in your life who depend on you to be the broken story. They cannot risk you changing. If you are "the bad situation," their lives are better than yours. Your healing and happiness make them the "situation." No one wants to claim the bottom rung. Your life becomes the very situation you tried to heal from, and now it confines you.

You will meet many people who need you to stay broken during your life. People who are afraid of you healing because if you heal, then what does that mean for them? If you listen closely, broken people tend to introduce themselves with situational labels like their relationship, health, or occupational status. This behavior demonstrates how the situation is ruling their lives and those "attached" to them. Their life stopped growing the day they became a victim of the situation. The longer they stay in that period, the harder it is for them to grow out of it.

We have all heard inspiring stories of people who lived through the worst of experiences and turned tragedy into something positive. Some of the most incredible work and legacy projects have come from those with the most difficult situations. Most of us know friends or family members who cling to yesterday's experiences and refuse to let go. A survivor regains power while the victim remains powerless.

What if we choose to look forward instead of being that person who lives in the past? What if everything that happened in your life gave you the strength to become "that inspiring story"? What if the situation was designed for you to be the solution to help others and share it with the world? If you change your perspective on why these things happened to you, it is easier to think about who loses if you don't win. Everyone loses. This is why we want to teach our children that situations cannot take us down—they only serve to build us up.

We move into the new behaviors we desire today by living today's story and leaving the past behind us. The past becomes truly the past, so we focus on building the future that we want. We can still honor the past and choose to live in the future. True love is to grow forward. It is a love of self and designing our life story. This is when everything begins to change. Life gets exciting when we step into the here and now. Here is where we have the power to control our outcome.

Being victimized is not a reflection of you. It has absolutely nothing to do with you. As you move through this book, you will start to identify what is yours to hold onto and what you can nicely hand back to its original owner. As humans, we like to carry baggage, but we are only responsible for our work. Once you create the "rules" for your designed life, people will automatically remove themselves who cannot comply with your new minimum standard. You don't have to do a thing. That is the true magic of this process. The minute you become that mirror for others' truth, people move to the sidelines and allow you to step boldly into your arena. Life was not designed to be a spectator sport, so let's get you in the game and living the life designed for you and by you.

Other people are not our projects, nor are we theirs. It is not our job to fix, change, parent, or raise anyone but ourselves and our children. There is no such thing as 50/50 in any relationship. Everyone needs to be operating from a complete one hundred percent when it comes to giving, receiving, and showing up as an independent and whole person. We are one hundred percent responsible for our side of living life. Meaning we are one hundred percent responsible for our happiness, our purpose, how we show up, and even our own pleasure. The idea of 50/50 throws way too much onto someone else's side. This idea of "you complete me" or "my better half" is a fallacy. Who wants to be operating from a place of "less than" or incomplete? Take a minute to think about this statement: *You complete me.*

Doesn't that sound exhausting? Not only do you have to figure out your life, but you are saddled with completing someone else's.

Often, we get into relationships where we start trying to fix people. Instead of accepting someone for who they are and operating from a place of acceptance, we take them on as our project and fall in love with their potential. Designing your own life means you get to create your own rules of the game based on what you want. The next step is to create your minimum standards. Establishing your boundaries allows you to bring people into your life without the need to change them. When you learn the skill of accepting people for who and where they are without judgment and without any responsibility to change them, you also stop creating resistance energy.

Designing Genius is about helping you decode where your choices will lead you and determining if that is where you want to go. If it is the wrong desired outcome, you can pivot by changing your choices. The beauty of this process is that Designing Genius is based on how you desire to feel. Your vision for your life is very different from mine, which is how life is meant to be. Despite what everyone wants us to believe, we are not meant for cookie-cutter living.

We can open any social media channel, and it appears that everyone except for us has a perfect life figured out. Our comparison thinking goes into overdrive, and it is tempting to start mimicking others' behaviors, trying to get the same results. With all the likes, posts, comments, and shares, it is easy to get caught up in the excitement of the possibility.

Whose Truth Is It Anyway?

Remember, with every action, there's an equal and opposite reaction. We often see someone living some aspect of a life we think we want but are only looking at the positive things on the surface. For every shiny object, there's a cost and a sacrifice. One of my greatest triumphs in business was a company that I built that was eventually acquired by Clorox. On the surface, things looked amazing, but there was a trade-off. It cost me my marriage. At the time, being a CEO and supporting my team was more important to me than my husband.

Now, this may sound cold. Through this process of building and selling a company, I later realized that although I told myself a million stories about how working around the clock was a requirement of the job, the truth is, I was giving the best parts of me to my company and team and the leftovers to my marriage. No matter how much my words were trying to tell a good story, my behavior and actions showed I valued the business more than my relationship. It got all my attention, energy, and thoughts and was the first oxygen mask I put on before anything or anyone else.

Does this make me a rotten person? No, it makes this my truth and one that I own. Now I've learned to move through my personal and professional life by clearly identifying what I value and the systems I need in place to pour daily into the things I value. When you know better, you can make better choices. That is what happened when I started making choices for a better future me. Designing Genius is about creating balance in the areas of life that are most important to you.

For anything to sustain and survive, it must be fed constantly, which we discuss later in this book about the Five Areas of Focus. What you do not feed, starves. I starved my marriage and fed the business. As I have gotten older and wiser, I have realized the ripple effect and responsibility those choices carry as they impact more than just me. Today I've learned better and show up more aligned with my truth.

This is what is meant by "be careful what you wish for." When looking at someone else's life, examine it from the proper lens. It's easy to say you want to look like a particular person until you learn they exercise two hours a day, follow a strict diet, and never eat pizza. That is where the cost comes into play.

A Peek Behind the Curtain

How often have you learned through the media that your favorite celebrity, influencer, athlete, or performer was involved in a scandal? Or that they have personal or relationship struggles that are never hinted at in their social media accounts? Or found other evidence not supporting the life they want you to see?

Social media can be used as a great equalizer when it comes to lifestyle perception. With just a few clicks and some amazing filters, everyone is living the ideal life. Or so it seems. As adults, it is our responsibility to design our lives based on reality. Stop worrying about online stylized photos and content and start leaning into the truth you want for your life.

We are so absorbed in taking food pictures, creating daily content, and obsessively scrolling that we are entirely disconnected from what is happening right in front of us. It has become normal to see two people at dinner looking down at their phones rather than looking across the table at one another. This is why New York City installed bumps in the sidewalks, to stop people from walking blindly into the street while looking down at their phones. Those who spend half their day looking down are missing the life happening right before them.

Do those millions of dollars or millions of followers still matter if the result is loneliness and misery? Of course not. We all want to live a well-designed life where we feel seen, heard, valued, and celebrated. When we start daydreaming about other people's "highlight reel," we are on a slippery slope that ends with a feeling of emptiness. We give power to a false narrative that robs us of joy. Instead, let's focus energy on designing exactly what brings and attracts the right type of people who value and celebrate us. Doesn't that sound way more productive and real?

Your Last Time

Please take a moment to slow down with me. What if you knew what you are doing right now was the last time you would do it? What if this was the last night you slept next to the person you love, the last time you had dinner with your parents, the last time you laughed with your best friend? The last time you were able to go to the gym, walk, or run? What if today was the last time you kissed a loved one goodbye?

What would you do differently if you knew this was the last time? Would you change your pace? Pay more attention to the tiny details like the touch of their lips, the way they tilt their head when they laugh, and the odd quirks that make them unique?

Take a moment to let those questions settle into your mind. In reality, someday an experience will happen for the last time. Most goodbyes happen before we realize they are happening. Pausing to reflect on this is not to create sadness but to draw awareness to how we can be more present and appreciate and value our current reality.

We have become a disposable society. We have falsely been told we can swipe left or right and replace people of substance based on a picture we see on a screen. We cannot easily replace an intimate lover or a life partner. The people who will roll up their sleeves through the hard times, understand our needs, and respect our dreams are not people we stumble upon. This is not how it works. Soul mates are made and not found. Finding someone willing to make a life with you is unique and incredibly valuable. The hard truth is we can never make new "old" friends. We miss these high-value relationships when we get blinded by the quick fix of the swiping nonsense that drives people to be lonelier than ever.

Here's the thing: Our mind has a funny way of disconnecting from the everyday details and taking for granted the real value of a life that matters. This is why learning to recognize how you feel and what feeds your desired life has the most significant impact on the life you design to live. Without a strong practice in place, these details get bulldozed over by the long list of superficial desires on which we place importance. We start doing life and stop living life. Our minds gloss over the details that make life feel amazing, like small acts of kindness, new connections, and feeling seen by another human. We are hardwired into a survival "pattern" of seeking out the negative. Meaning it is easier for our mind to find fault than it is to find pleasure. It is how we are trained to survive through our early years of development. But these survival skills rob us of those small, perfect moments that bring us joy.

Creating your genius life is a five-step process that empowers you to show up to your life more intentionally, impactfully, and energetically. Once you have these five steps down, making decisions regarding your time, energy, and focus becomes easier because you have clarity around the aspects of your life that are most important to you.

Tara's Story
Prior to meeting Amilya last July and working with her shortly after, Tara was in a constant struggle of finding her narrative, balancing her day, and feeling exhausted. She was working so hard and yet felt so unproductive. It felt like beating a dead horse daily. Read on to find out how Designing Genius tools have impacted Tara's life.

How did you try to fix the situation?
I have paid tens of thousands of dollars on programs, courses, masterminds, even one-on-ones. Even just prior to meeting Amilya, I paid for a program worth almost $10,000 with zero results. It wasn't for a lack of effort on my end, it was because I was aligning with the wrong people. People who couldn't see my gifts, my zone of genius, and know exactly what I need to unlock more of it.

What solution or tool did you use based on Designing Genius or something you heard from Amilya Antonetti?
I met Amilya Antonetti through an app called Clubhouse where's she's often a guest speaker in large rooms, shifting people within minutes and solving heavy issues that take therapists years to resolve. I was blown away! I learned with small behavior modifications, our lives dramatically change! I heard her speak in New York during 2021, and I knew that she was the one who would help me break free from this box I felt confined in. She was different, her passion could be felt through her speaking, her authenticity was powerful, and I watched her own her gifts with pride and a sense of duty and service to others. She truly loves and is deeply passionate about helping people find purpose and fulfillment simply by shifting people's behavior.

How long did it take for you to see a change or result?

I joined her program and week by week, I started to experience massive shifts in my productivity and energy. She has so many tools that are incredible, but her calendar and the "should and should nots" have changed my life. I implemented her tools and within weeks, I started to notice that I was no longer feeding into what wasn't serving me. I no longer needed to chase or wait for information, and most importantly, I've attracted all the right people who appreciate and respect my zone of genius as well as my gifts. I no longer strive for perfection and have found I spend more time in recovery rather than strain. So many changes—so many tools! So much growth, super-fast!

How is this situation for you today?

I look back on where I was last July, and what a difference!! I've managed to scale my current business and clients. I opened another company, launched a new podcast, and unlocked so many new opportunities and connections with so many people aligned in my arena who seek me rather than me seeking them. Amilya Antonetti has created a course that is challenging and yet so rewarding! There are fundamental tools and deep dives that will absolutely and unequivocally change your life if you are willing to do some work. Best decision in my career thus far. I am so grateful that our paths crossed in our journeys and look forward to what's ahead.

Unlocking Tool

Every day, hour, and second we have on this planet matters. Our goal with Designing Genius is to maximize every single moment we have left and live a life of intention and purpose. As you will discover, the work starts from within, and it is an internal process that reverberates outward into every area of your life. To reinforce the message that the time is NOW to get started, let's begin with a little game to see why time is of the essence.

Time Truth Calculator Game
This game allows you to calculate how much time you have left on this planet based on the 2022 average life span of seventy-two years. With fifty-two weeks in a year, your lifetime spans 3,744 weeks. You can run the numbers for your age, and in the meantime, here are a few examples to give you a snapshot.

- A twenty-one-year-old has lived 1,092 weeks and has 2,652 weeks left.
- A thirty-five-year-old has lived 1,820 weeks and has 1,924 weeks left.
- A forty-five-year-old has lived 2,340 weeks and has 1,404 weeks left.
- A fifty-five-year-old has lived 2,860 weeks and has 884 weeks left.
- A sixty-five-year-old has lived 3,380 weeks and has 364 weeks left.

This exercise brings things into focus, right? Why would you spend your last 884 weeks on earth with anyone who does not think you are the most amazing human on the planet? Why would you waste a single moment only seeing the negative? Valuing the wrong things? Dwelling in the past? And spending time with *anyone* who does not put in *effort*. If you take nothing more from this book than this one *fact*, then you are faster than most.

Time is our greatest equalizer, and when we see how fast time flies and start to realize how little time we have with our parents, lovers, children, and friends, the appreciation, quality, and gratitude of those relationships grow. Fault-finding, living by default, or living someone else's design no longer becomes an option. Remove yourself from anyone who lives their life by looking in the rearview mirror. Yes, we love those who have been part of our life story to this point, but the remaining weeks, months, and years of your life that are in front of you are the most important. Anyone from your early chapters who truly loved you would encourage you to live in the present. Live NOW—it's over before you know it. We have ZERO time to waste on negative energy when positive energy is just as available and abundant.

The Time Truth Calculator brings clarity and eases decision-making. If we have less than one thousand weeks left, why would we spend another week in a dead-end job, a lonely relationship, or with people who do not value and celebrate us? This exercise impacts our perspective so that NOW is the time to take that vacation, see the wonders of the world, call that person we have neglected, and let bygones be bygones. Stop putting things off by thinking things like:

- *When I lose weight, I will start . . .*
- *When I find my life partner, I will . . .*
- *When I make a million dollars, I will . . .*
- *When the kids get out of college then . . .*
- *When I retire . . .*

None of us have time to waste. The time is NOW to start designing your genius life. When you identify your areas of focus and utilize the tools in this book, it is one hundred percent impossible not to get closer to getting everything you want. Ready to get started?

Chapter 2

A Game with No Rules

Your life is made up of *choices*. This may sound super obvious, but so many of us live as if we don't have them. We don't consider what we stand to lose or gain by certain decisions we make. We forget to weigh the risk versus the reward and then wonder why our life feels out of alignment to the person we dreamed of becoming. Designing Genius is the awakening to that awareness that may be missing. It puts you into the driver's seat to plug in the GPS coordinates of where you want to go, so you are no longer the passenger on someone else's journey.

As you learned in the exercise from the Time Truth Calculator, none of us have extra time to spare. We are all on a countdown to our last weeks on this planet. This is not to cause anxiety or worry, but to inspire action so we can maximize the time we have left. We want to infuse the right energy and effort into how we choose to spend our days. This is how we align the goals and visions we have for ourselves, our family, and our careers with how we show up in the world. It is quite simple when we put in the work. Instead of living on autopilot, we are following a perfectly designed blueprint created by us and for us.

This is exponentially better than running around in reaction mode and fulfilling other people's agendas because we haven't taken the time to identify what is important to us. This "spray and pray" method is like throwing a bunch of things up against a wall and hoping something will stick. It is exhausting. It is ineffective. And it leaves a lot of room for regret.

People can dramatically change the trajectory of their lives with just a few easy behavior modifications. Through a better understanding of "self-"made lifestyle changes, it's possible to strengthen relationships, grow your business, and reconcile with childhood trauma. Why? Because when we design the rules for OUR game, the rules do the work for us.

The Designing Genius process is the greatest weapon we have to combat distraction and negativity because it organizes our life in a way that keeps us focused on the right things and eliminates those things no longer serving us. With our standards in place, the wrong people and the wrong opportunities will eliminate themselves. They will either choose to step up and meet you where you are, or they will choose not to play your game. It is like a new twist on an old saying: "Grow and choose happy with me or get out of my way." This becomes the glue that allows you to live a beautiful life.

Love Story vs. Life Story

Life is not a fairy tale. I know, I know…we have been shown so many fairy tales where Prince Charming or the beautiful princess walks into our life and POOF! Happiness and bliss arrive with them.

I can tell you with total certainty this is simply not how it works. Nothing outside of "self" brings happiness. It is a choice only you can make for you. You can't buy it, and no one can give it to you. Open any media page or magazine and you will find another celebrity, comedian, entertainer, or big CEO who has all the money and "things" but is going through another divorce, business dispute, or scandal. Those external possessions cannot fill the internal void or gap occurring within them.

Many people collect things, cars, houses, and possessions to try and fill an emptiness deep inside. I call these folks "collectors". It doesn't matter what they choose as their "outside of self" item, it never feeds the internal appetite. The adrenaline or dopamine hit that comes with that new bright and shining object is fleeting and sends the person off to pursue the next possession they think will fill the void.

Whether the goal is a big house, a purse that is so desirable that it has a waitlist, or a few extra zeros in the bank account, the feeling that comes with getting *it* is never big enough to create what we truly desire. The "things" cannot fix what is broken inside of you. The "never enough" race has no finish line. It is a hamster wheel that just goes around and around. The pleasure that follows each acquisition gets less and less as we discover the hollowness that comes with empty pursuits. Trying to heal loneliness or pain externally is self-medicating whether you choose drugs, alcohol, shopping, sex, or over-working. The road to happiness, fulfillment, and Designing Genius is an inside job. No one can do the work for us. And no one can give it to you.

Let's get very real for a second and discuss an amazing truth. Your presence on this planet is no accident. You've been customized by your Creator, the universe, or whatever belief system you subscribe to. What I know for sure is you are absolutely here for a reason, and you have been given a gift that is your genius. This is necessary for your life's purpose. You are not a carbon copy of any other creation for good reason. The goal is to unlock how to get inside of our internal self and locate where you connect to happiness. I refer to this as "rooted" like the roots of a tree. The roots grow first under the soil before the first bud pushes through to the surface and becomes the tree it was created to be. We are also like a tree. We need to locate the seeds that formed the roots of what brings our true happiness.

Many of us are miles away from family or a reliable support system, which can be a problem because we were not taught how to build one to help us thrive. Nor were we taught how to pick the people who are a good fit for our desired lives. It's been friendship by default. We make a few friends in school who we try to hold onto, but for the most part, we outgrow these friendships. These friendships can sometimes sustain but often lack the substance required to evolve. We try to fill the void with the "parent pool." These are the folks we meet through our kids, and these, too, are surface-level relationships that entertain us at best but are not chosen with any intention of a bigger life by design. Without a support system, we eventually crash and burn. There is a very good reason why they say, "There is no solo in success."

The self-awareness and clarity of one's wants and needs, as an individual, a partnership, on a team, or as a leader are blurred if we don't know what we want. It is impossible to define what we want and need from others if we have not defined what we want for ourselves. Designing Genius will help you create a measurement to determine if you are getting closer to your desired outcome, or farther away. Most of us are guessing and hoping it works out. Until it doesn't. Then we desperately try to stop the downward spiral without even knowing what the heck we are trying to hold onto.

Keep in mind that we, all of us, cling tightly to what we know. Even if we consciously know what we are holding tightly to, is not in our best interest. We hold what is familiar to us. This is the fundamental behavior that stops people from leaving bad jobs and relationships and releasing destructive habits. Subconsciously, we would rather deal with the devil we know than step into the uncertainty of what will happen if we let go. Fear of the unknown has many people trapped within its grasp.

From the day we are born, we are experimenting with these different types of relationships. As children, it is with parents, teachers, and classmates. As adults, it is with work colleagues, romantic relationships, and friendships. We are seeking acceptance and connection at every stage of our life. And at the same time, we embark on a hero's journey that begins the day we are born. We face challenges, fears, obstacles, and adventures. We are offered opportunities for transformation at every turn but must be willing to assume risk. And like a hero, many of us start out by seeking a guide, but without a strong internal compass, that strategy does not work.

A relationship between you and your guide, boss, partner, or best friend is only as strong as the right pairing. The energetic alignment between two people starts with respecting and understanding the journey each person is on. This is why we start with self. If we don't know our own priorities and standards, how can we communicate them to others? The answer is that we can't. It is unrealistic to expect people to guess what we need, want, or desire. Their rules of life may be different from ours. They may be in a different stage of their life. They may be focused on family, while we are focused on work. They may need daily contact, while we need space. The intersection within these relationships comes by doing the exercises in this book.

Designing Genius not only helps us understand what game we are playing, but what we hope to get from our current experience. It identifies the stakes of the game that occur at every milestone, so we can decide if the cost is worth the reward. One person may be playing for power or prestige, while another is looking for connection and community. How we establish and follow the rules feeds into the results we ultimately receive.

Here is one of those hard truths: Everyone is playing the game for something, for some value. We all want to believe the story that we are generous people and give for the sake of giving. We want to believe that others randomly give for no reason, but let's decode what is really going on. You and others give with some expectation and some idea of what will happen in return. Often this trade is unspoken and not clear. We "hope" it all works out in our favor. However, it rarely does, and not because we do not deserve the very best. It doesn't work out because we are guessing and hoping. Designing a genius life is about developing structure and guidelines. Even generous and loving people need to understand that what they are putting into the world is received with the intentions they wanted. Until we do this work, we are spraying and praying and on a road to burnout.

When what we give is received with respect, value, and acknowledgment of our gifts then life starts to move closer to ebb and flow. Our giving has an expectation that it will be received with the acknowledgement it deserves. This is not tit for tat, which is scorekeeping that destroys relationships. Scorekeeping is a behavior that demonstrates a person is more married to keeping tabs and is looking for evidence to prove they are winning. Whereas the measurement we want is about respect and the value to be seen, heard, and recognized for feeding into the relationship.

How someone really feels about you cannot be measured in the beginning of a partnership, job, or friendship. This is referred to as the honeymoon phase, or the first three to six months of the relationship. In this phase, you are tested, knowingly or unknowingly, to see when your minimum standards are met. If you want to see the true character of someone, look at the endings. Look at how they ended their last job, their last board seat role, their last relationship. Look at the way someone ends, and it tells you exactly who they are. If you look at yourself and how you left your last relationship, it gives huge insight to your own beliefs and behaviors. The beginnings are easy; the endings are where we are tested and stretched to reveal our true character and values.

Most people have at least one heartbreak story of a bad breakup. Most of us, if we reflect back, would have never imagined the person we cared about, who claimed to care about us, could treat us so awfully, but they did. If we were able to data mine into their past, I bet we would find a pattern of the same behavior of where the relationship started great but ended with the same negativity. To predict the future, look at someone's history. A person of great character and substance puts in the same effort in ending things as they do in starting them.

The rules and strategies for relationships get more advanced as we move through the rites of passage of our life. People move in and out of our lives on a regular basis. They remove themselves based on their choice to honor or not to honor our rules of the game. That's on them, not us. People demonstrate their decision to be part of our journey based on the evidence they present to us on an ongoing basis. This is displayed by the choices they make according to the boundaries we have established. These rules and guidelines are essential on our journey toward happiness and fulfillment.

For example, if you value punctuality and make it known that honoring your time and others' time is one way you measure value in a relationship, then someone who is always late is operating by a different set of rules. It sets the foundation for the conversation that says, "Listen, I see lots of value in who you are, but I see we are misaligned in our relationship with time. If it's not important enough for you to be on time for our calls and meetings, then I do not foresee our relationship getting stronger or sustaining. I have a minimum standard that when someone I value is late two or three times then I begin stepping back and limiting my effort in that relationship. I respect you and want you to know this is how I am feeling and the choices that I see in front of me. Can you share how you see it?"

This creates a dialogue for two people to determine if they can develop a life story together or if they should limit their interaction and agree the relationship is not of high value. Together they can agree to go their separate ways and respect each other's desire for a different lifestyle. It is okay to care for someone and still be glad they are not in your life. Your love for someone is not the strongest variable in deciding whether someone should remain in your life. Your minimum standards have more than one variable to consider for the formula that defines a healthy relationship. When you start Designing Genius, you may find yourself asking for the very first time, "What do I want for my life?" Once we remove the fairytale notions and get down to finding the evidence of genius living then it is the awareness of self that holds the answers to our highest and greatest life.

Understanding Resistance

To better understand resistance, let's set the foundation first with the understanding that everything has energy. There is a quote often attributed to Albert Einstein, although unsubstantiated, that says, "Everything is energy, and that's all there is to it. Match the frequency of the reality you want, and you cannot help but get that reality. It can be no other way. This is not philosophy. This is physics." If everything has energy, it's important to know that there are two sides to energy. One side controls energy, and the other side generates energy. Both sides of the energy equation are needed and equally important. When we are resisting, we are trying to control the energy.

By nature, our thoughts and behaviors take the path of least resistance. This starts in childhood with what we know and what we learn. We begin to believe that what comes easiest is best, so it takes awareness and desire to challenge those beliefs and decisions. Instead of building an autonomous life full of passion, motivation, and inspiration, we continue down a road that feels unfulfilling. Success of any kind is found outside our comfort zone because success is not a comfortable process. This is why we developed Designing Genius to create the touchstones that let you know you are moving and growing.

As a child, you may have learned you could skip brushing your teeth and get five more minutes of playtime because no one checked. As a teen, you may have learned you could wait until the night before a test to cram and still get a passing grade. These small life moments allow for the least resistance for a short-term gain, whereas the highest resistance is found with a long-term gain.

There is a behavior game often found in elementary schools that is based on the Stanford Marshmallow experiment and the Cookie Study. Kids are asked to choose if they want one cookie or marshmallow now or three at the end of the day. These studies found that the kids who chose the longer-term gain, resulting in delayed gratification and willpower, were 70 percent more successful in school and life than those who went for the short-term reward. The more practice we get in managing and strategizing resistance energy for long-term rewards, the more capacity we have for sustainable success. Most people are NOT aware that one of the biggest skills to success is consciously building a relationship with resistance and recovery energy and intentionally building this capacity. These are crucial life skills for success of any kind.

Our resistance is fundamentally rooted in not being able or willing to deal with the negative experiences in our life *as it is*. There is a strong emphasis on "as it is" because there is much that goes into decoding "what is." This means strengthening our awareness that something is always happening, and what we think is happening is only our point of view and perspective. There is an entirely different story being written from someone else's point of view.

When we think our point of view is right, we are in the experience and subconsciously committed to being right. When this happens, we have already lost. We lost half of the story being written. We lost the connection to the other person within the experience because we are resistant to the idea of other ideas or solutions. The ability to move into someone else's experience of the story they are having changes the game and our ability to rise to our best in every relationship. When we are present in what is happening all around us then we are the rudder of our own ship and can steer anywhere we wish to go. Now that is a powerful place to live. Choosing to serve others while we are at our best allows us to live one experience at a time.

Happiness depends on our awareness and abilities to know what is happening, as well as the skills to handle and make choices. Then we must be willing to let go of that which is not serving us or getting us to the desired outcome. This is the release of resistance energy. At the same time, we want to lean into the choices and mindset that do give us what we want and enjoy. Someone famous said, "What you resist will persist." The goal is to break this behavioral cycle.

To free ourselves from any guilt (this, too, is resistant energy), we must understand that our initial state of being comes from our survival state of self-protection. This is where we all start. We learn denial for self-protection. We also learn to paint the story that feels better to us. Many live their entire life holding onto the story that makes them feel better and not the reality of what is happening. Stories are rooted in emotion. The emotion we attach to anything gives that thing meaning. It is the meaning we give something that determines how we feel.

Keep in mind that true growth hurts. The hurt must be transformed into harmony or "flow" energy. When we live in this state, we attract more of what we want. This self-care and self-intended energy propels us to move away from the vicious cycle of attaching what things mean to emotions and being so married to the outcomes that there is no room for things to be what they are.

Most people fight against what they don't want to feel. This, in turn, brings more of what we don't want to feel to the surface. Simon Sinek says this best when he teaches that the mind cannot properly interpret negative language. His example to prove that our mind cannot function in negative thoughts is by asking people to not think of an elephant. Try it.

How did your mind do? Failed, right? Because it is impossible to "not think" about what we tell our minds not to think about. Our brains don't recognize the instructions of "do not". Instead, it brings forward the exact thing we were trying not to do. It's about learning to think and speak in alignment with how our minds work.

Who wants to build a life cycle of pain? We unintentionally hold onto feelings of hurt, sorrow, anxiety, or anger. We rely on willpower to get us from one decision to the next. Instead of pulling what we want toward us, we make it hard by pushing away everything we don't want, and in turn, it comes more often, because what we resist always persists. This is the resistance energy keeping us in place.

Let's free ourselves to move toward a better way, to think of what we want, create the positive frequency, and move toward flow by attracting this same energy and releasing anything that does not serve us in a positive way. Let's rid ourselves of things bringing negative resistance energy into our life. And let's create the rules that help us communicate and connect in a way where belonging and accepting the energy of self are at the core.

Cory's Story

Cory was facing the challenge of her youngest son, a sophomore in high school, presenting her with his desire to move in with her ex-husband, his dad, to finish out his last three years of schooling. He listed the advantages of going to a bigger school that might offer more opportunities for him toward a basketball scholarship. There was also some tension at her home between her son and husband (stepdad) and different points of view with chores, responsibilities, etc. Read on to find out how Designing Genius tools helped Cory's process and communicate throughout this situation.

What solution or tool did you use based on Designing Genius or something you heard from Amilya Antonetti?
Devastated with thinking I would lose precious time with my "baby", I could not see the importance and significance in him wanting to make this transition. Through the clarity of rites of passage and how important it is for each of us to "go through" different levels of learning before we move to the next step in our life journey, I was able to release the sadness and fear I had for my child moving out. Understanding the importance of a young man desiring to feel the bond of another man and have the freedom to "push back" against another man—instead of the constant pressure of controlling or suppressing certain emotions with his mom—was an important step in his life that I was not honoring. I was being selfish, wanting my baby boy to stay close where I could protect him from failure, bad decisions, etc. I would have been stealing the opportunity from him to grow from these situations.

Most importantly, I possibly would have been creating feelings of resentment from him by trying to control his actions at an age when hormones and lack of maturity often come second to common sense.

How long did it take for you to see a change or result?
About three weeks. I was still sad and fearful for about four days. He knew I did not want it to happen, but he was surprised by my willingness to support him and to sit down to figure out a plan of when it would happen, what classes would he need to take, how would we change the visitation schedule. I let him know it was okay that I did not like it, but I am always here to support him through something. These are his choices, which come with consequences or results. We went over some of the pros and cons—his friends, his work, his athletics. I tried very hard to remain neutral, letting him do most of the talking and me just guiding here and there.

I asked my son for an update on whether he was still looking at moving to his dad's. Unsolicited, with no coercing, he said that he had thought more about it and after weighing the things we talked about, he decided to stay with me. My heart could have burst out of my chest. I was so happy but careful to show moderate joy, explaining to him that it was his choice but that I was grateful to be able to spend more time with him.

How is this situation for you today?
Now, even though I loved his decision to stay, I had to re-weigh what I learned about rites of passage and understand how I can be a loving, protective mother but still give him room to grow as a young man should. I have since had meaningful, difficult,

> intimate discussions with my husband to assist in him understanding the expectations I have as his role as a participant stepdad. This has provided desired boundaries for him and my son and structure that gives my son more clarity of where their relationship is. Now I enjoy a win/win from both my husband and my son.

Unlocking Tool

As humans, if we desire something, the evidence of that desire exists in our life so we can communicate to others it has value. In relationships, partnerships, and with employees, we want people whose actions match their words. Remember: How you do one thing is how you do everything. Intentionality and action are the proof that the follow-through exists beyond words.

For example, if someone says they want to live a healthy, physically fit lifestyle, then there should be evidence to support that the statement is true. This might be time blocked off on the calendar, a gym membership, a change in food habits, or home gym equipment. If this is a genuine desire, there is proof; if not, it is simply not true.

If an employee says they want to start speaking at company events, then when they are allowed to present their ideas at company meetings, they should speak up. If their manager offers them time off to attend Toastmasters, they will sign up and mark the time off on their calendar. The proof of its importance will exist.

How to Play

This exercise allows you to evaluate if your words match your current activities. Often, we say one thing but do not follow through on our actions. Get a piece of paper, a pen, and have your cell phone, planner, and calendar available.

Gameplay:
1. Begin the exercise by taking five to seven minutes to list the most important things in your life regarding relationships, hobbies, work, and self-care.
2. Get out your phone and look for proof in your calendar that any of these items are important.
3. Next, go through your list and identify evidence in your life that your actions match your words.

This exercise is so important because we do not want to be serving others and ourselves with empty words. When we say we love or desire something, it needs to be more than lip service. Think about it in a romantic situation. We don't want someone just to say, "I love you." We want the evidence to show up in other ways. Thoughtful notes, kindness to our friends, calling to check in, and a shoulder to cry on are ways that people demonstrate they care and that we are valuable to them.

Chapter 3

What Is Designing Genius?

When was the last time you purchased a new game and didn't read the rules? Or took on a new job and didn't inquire about office hours, benefits, and how to request time off? From the time we are born to the day we die, we are learning new rules from our parents, teachers, government, and bosses.

Rules provide an agreement of understanding. If the word "boundaries" sits better with your spirit, then use that terminology. What we know for sure is that as humans we thrive in structure. If we want to build anything, we must first set the foundation. The rules and boundaries are part of setting a strong foundation for us to build upon. It's part of the foundation's strength, and thus the sustainability. Many people have researched the need for structure when raising children. They need these rules and boundaries to know what's expected of them. This structure gives them a sense of security, lessens anxiety so they know what's coming next, and provides a foundation from which to grow. This baseline for optimal growing instills a sense of dependability so they know what to do, why, and when to do it.

So why not have this structure in our own lives? In our relationships? The pre-work for Designing Genius is building awareness, structure, and rules of the game so everyone feels safer and more dependable in their lives and their relationships.

Think about it: All sports have rules that define what is allowed or not allowed for the game. Break a rule, and you are out of bounds, penalized, or kicked out of the game. Can you imagine if the players didn't know or understand the rules? They would be on the field guessing and confused when they got tossed out of the game for not knowing the rules.

How many relationships are operating the exact same way? Rules, spoken and unspoken, are the core that governs anything and everything. When someone pushes against what we believe these rules to be, we hand out consequences. The problem is, if no one knows what our rules are, they have no idea the consequences we have attached to "rule-breaking". And if we do not know our own rules, we send out mixed messages that are inconsistent and then get frustrated about the results.

Can you see part of the problem? The rules of the game are not clearly defined.

Even the rules of war, or international humanitarian law (as it is known formally) are a set of international rules that are laid out to maintain some humanity in armed conflicts to save lives and reduce suffering.

So, if each of these areas of interaction has rules and guidelines, don't you think the most important relationships in our life should have "rules of the game" to set up each person for sustainable success? From friendships, colleagues, and neighbors, to family, relationships, and children, we need to know how to communicate our expectations to ourselves and to others. This becomes the MVP (minimum viable product) of what we will and will not accept in our lives.

What Is Designing Genius?

A recent study on couples who sustained a relationship for more than ten years said the number one variable in their sustainability and joy was the presence of structure and guidelines around "how to fight".[1] They were the couples that stood the test of time. This is why it's so important to build your own "rules of the game" and how to communicate them to those in your circle of trust. Learning how to love and how to handle conflict are critical life skills to maintain happiness with other people.

When I am working with families or children under the age of eighteen, my first question to the child is, "Do you know what the rules are to play your favorite sport?" I listen to how they so easily explain the rules of the sport they are interested in. I ask if knowing the rules makes them better at their sport, which they agree that it does. Next, I ask if they know what the rules are to be successful in their family. For this question they always have less clarity. They often know some of the things they could do that would get them into trouble within the family, but that is about it. I help the child recognize they do not have the same level of clarity about the family rules and boundaries like they do about the sport they just described. This is enlightening for their parents who are observing.

I do this same exercise between employees and their boss and in personal relationships. This Q&A quickly identifies that as leaders, partners, and parents we make up rules randomly and don't stick to them. Our rules are not clear or understood. We do not get a buy-in from the other person to acknowledge the penalty. Rewards change randomly or are nonexistent. Ninety percent of the clients who hire me to improve their personal and professional relationships have zero structure or rules of the game in place. Everyone is randomly

---

[1] Betuel, Emma. "Landmark Study on 11,196 Couples Pinpoints What Dating Apps Get So Wrong." Inverse, July 27, 2020. https://www.inverse.com/mind-body/dating-study-predicts-happy-relationships.

hoping it all works out and that their children and partners will figure it out.

Sounds crazy, right? Some of the best couple pairings with the most potential to build a genius life destroyed the relationship because they believed in mind reading, deflection, avoidance, and guessing. It is such a waste of precious energy and is extremely hurtful when one or both people are solving partnership problems in their head alone. They have no idea what either of them are building toward or why. They have no tools about how to communicate their needs or share what brings them joy. They add kids into the mix thinking it will calm things down, but it just adds to the noise. The frustration increases because everyone is having conversations within their own head and not with the people that can help solve it. They take it for as long as they can and then burn out.

Here is the kicker: They leave this relationship without learning why it didn't work. They blame surface level things without realizing it was a lack of life skills and behavioral tools that created the issues. They leave this relationship, this employee, this job and start new with someone else. Guess what? They have the same problems. They create the same patterns. As soon as the honeymoon phase and newness wear off, the same old issues appear. Why? Because there are no life skills, partner skills, and rules of the game for success that sets a foundation for the relationship to build upon. The tools to guide the growth, value, and rewards to celebrate are not clear and understood. People are trying to have amazing and meaningful relationships by hoping it works out, until it doesn't. Guessing will never put someone in the winner's circle.

When we understand the power in our connections and the need for belonging that all humans have, it becomes clear that yesterday's teaching and rules are not robust enough to grow us into the life we desire. Yesterday's knowledge and thinking will not meet the needs and wants of those we choose to love, today. I promise that once you live one day by the rules you need to live life to the fullest, you will never go back to the guessing game. These rules become more invaluable for us and for those we choose to be in our closest and most trusted circle.

The rules of the game become the glue that holds us together. Instead of spending so much energy struggling to get what we want and need, the rules do the heavy lifting. The relief felt is exponential. The room we have for what we value is beyond imaginable. Once we stop investing time, energy, money, and resources into false assumptions, we can move away from misalignment and energy vampires. Life starts to feel a whole lot less frustrating. Fundamentally at our core, all people are hardwired to connect and belong. Without it, we are slowly dying from within whether we realize it or not.

Designing Genius

Now that we have determined that living a life by design is the key to unlocking what we want from life, let's create your compass. It is going to take some work, a new way of thinking, and a bit of willpower to push through resistance. But if we want different results, we have to do something different.

Starting now, we are going to choose the game we want to play moving forward. In the coming chapters, we will build upon the concept of the perfect game. It's all designed one hundred percent by you and for you. The right people for your life will choose to play the game with you, and those who do not like the rules, or your minimum standard of effort required, will not play. Your Designing Genius game will include the following:

- **Your One Word:** This is the theme for your game. Your word sets the overarching feel or energy intention for the game.

- **Five Areas of Focus:** This is what happens between the start and finish lines of the game—the overall journey. These are the most important mile markers in your life right now.
- **Primary Ingredients:** These live within your five areas of focus and are the evidence that let you know you are heading in the right direction.
- **Should and Should Nots:** These provide the instruction manual and overall rules for your game.
- **Your Perfect Day:** This is proof you have won the game and provides the blueprint for others to help you succeed.

Fun fact: Every component of the Designing Genius game is created by you and for you. Playing this game makes you the ultimate winner, but there will be other winners as well. Those who choose to participate in your life of genius will get the best version of you. Your personal, professional, and romantic relationships will be stronger than ever.

Before we get started, I want to make sure we are all playing with the same end goal in mind. You may have been telling yourself for many years that "you just want to be happy." In theory, that probably sounds great. It sounds better than being sad, mad, depressed, or upset. So, maybe like most other people, you've been chasing "happiness". And like most other people, you've probably experienced it in spurts.

Properly defined, "happiness" implies a current state of satisfaction or fortune. It's temporary. This is why you can be happy when you buy something new on Friday and feel totally different on Saturday. Or be in a terrible relationship with someone but stick around because the moments of happiness keep you engaged.

It seems strange to pursue an emotional state that is fleeting and implies that the rest of your life is less positive. What if instead of seeking "happy", our ultimate goal was "peace"? What if you could feel harmony in all your personal relationships?

Properly defined, "peace" is a lack of conflict between yourself and other people. Put into practice, it allows you to feel calm and handle stress. There's a tranquility that comes with inner peace that is transferable to every area of your life. The Should and Should Nots exercises in this book help maintain and protect that inner peace, so that other people and things do not put us into a state of chasing how we want to feel in our life.

Are You a Fault Finder?

We must intentionally learn new thinking and behaviors that guide us into the life we choose to live—not default into a victim mentality rooted in things that randomly happen beyond our control. This is a false belief or misconception. We control what we think by what we feed our minds and thoughts. If we put garbage into our heads like fault and negativity, we get the garbage of feeling negative, less than, and not good enough. Fault finders must understand that what they see in others is a projection of self. We cannot see what does not exist within us. We find fault due to an unhealed and insecure place growing from inside.

The "fault finder" mentality destroys happiness and peace. If we live the bulk of our day finding fault in ourselves and others, that feels awful. Peace cannot grow from a negatively planted thought. Plant seeds of fault finding, and they grow negativity, shame, and pain. Plant seeds of gratitude, and they grow to love, belonging, and knowing.

What would happen if we flipped the script and refused to feed the fault finding behavior? That behavior would starve and stop. What if we began practicing finding the positive things in ourselves, the people we spend time with, and our lives?

This is the foundation of gratitude practice. To intentionally notice the small details that feel good. To not only identify the little things that make our hearts leap but hold a moment in time to celebrate them. Yes, gratitude is born in thoughts as simple as "I love that first perfect cup of coffee in the morning. I feel the excitement in my spirit the minute I smell it. That first sip tells me I am alive and wakes into an opportunity of an entire beautiful, amazing day."

Now, having this moment delivered by someone who loves you is priceless. But what happens when you rush by this moment or forget that this small act of self-love or partnership love touches your soul? Even worse, what happens when this act of kindness and love is not seen, appreciated, or valued? What we do not respect and celebrate, we will lose. Many of us take moments that once created joy for granted, and what we do not value goes away.

We stay where we are until we honor the details of today. Why would our life give us more if we do not appreciate what we already have? Happiness is not about being happy when we get to another destination. Happiness is found in the details of where we are right now and in being so deeply grateful. Remember, wherever you are today, it is likely that you are already living someone else's dream life.

Take a moment to sit with this thought: *We are living someone's dream life*, and that alone is a reason to be grateful for where we are. Love yourself and your life now, and the door to tomorrow opens. If we live our life looking for fault and wishing for someone else's life, we stay stuck in the past and live the same negative frequency day in and day out.

We have all met these people. They have so many things right in front of them to be so grateful for, and they choose misery because their thoughts convince them that "here" is not good enough. No amount of abundance or good fortune will change their mindset because they have wired their brain to find fault first. These fault finders are energy suckers, and they zap positivity and joy right out of the air.

Life becomes a manifestation of what is at the root of our thinking. Change the root thinking, glue the new practice into place, and life begins to feel dramatically different. Once we feel different, the world starts to deliver different outcomes. It sounds simple, but it is not. It does, however, begin with one simple choice: To choose gratitude. When you see fault, switch your focus to asking, "Does this thought or action bring any value to my overall desired genius living life?" If the answer is "no," then switch the fault focus to gratitude. I remember asking my grandmother how she slept next to my grandfather, who snored loudly. She answered that the nights he was not home, she missed him. For years after he passed, she said she would give anything to hear his loud snoring for just one more night.

The next time you catch yourself finding fault in the small things a loved one does, try pausing and holding space for just a moment to recognize the value and positive things this person adds to your life. Turning your mind's attention to positivity and gratitude is an easy way to refocus your mind. Flip the script and watch your life and the lives of those you love grow before your eyes.

Our mind is the most powerful tool we have. Without learning how to use and care for it properly, it's like handing someone a loaded gun. It would be dangerous to pick up a loaded gun and whirl it around while learning how to use it, right? We know that a weapon requires training to use and respect for its ability to inflict pain. Our mind is more powerful than a loaded weapon, and it can cause both pain and healing. This is why I walk clients through the "last time" life exercise from Chapter One.

When we connect with our last time, we can choose how to use our minds positively. We can have healthy and happy relationships and create respect, communication, gratitude, trust, intimacy, and commitment. A genius life allows us to take a strong audit of our behaviors to become more firmly grounded in building the system and tools we need for the life we desire. We learn to value what has real meaning to how we feel in life. It allows us to attach to every moment and treat it like it may be the last time. This frees our energy and enables us to navigate around regret.

You will learn how to create the rules of YOUR game to guide you toward the outcomes you want in your personal, professional, and family life. We must understand the gap present in our lives today from where we are to where we want to be. Then we can implement the process to build the stepping stones forward in our growth.

We only have one life. It is our life to design as we desire. We have been given a gift. We can open it early or late in life, but it is our gift to open it. If we do not open it and design our life, then it will be designed for us. If we hope someone comes along and makes these decisions for us, we better be careful about what we wish for. We will end up in a life that does not fit. We will wake up one day living a life we never wanted or intended. Not choosing is a choice. There is nothing lonelier than living someone else's life. There are so many tools we can use for living a genius life. Define the rules of your game to create harmony for you and those important relationships in your life.

CHOOSE joy and watch your life change.

Charleson's Story
Charleson went through a painful divorce a few months ago. Although it was amicable and they are still friends, it was very hurtful because he wanted to stay married. Read on to find out how Charleson used the Designing Genius tools to create self-care during a difficult time in his life.

How did you try to fix the situation?
I tried suppressing my emotions while still being available to my ex during the process.

What solution or tool did you use based on Designing Genius or something you heard from Amilya Antonetti?
I learned from Amilya that I must measure my return on investment (ROI) on how much access and energy I am giving to others. I had to be honest with my feelings by asking myself whether those interactions were serving me or hurting me.

How long did it take for you to see a change or result?
The change was immediate. It did not require an emotional revolution or denial. I just needed to take into account how I felt and align my boundaries, thoughts, and actions with that and my values.

How is this situation for you today?
Being true to myself allowed me to simultaneously embrace the healing process while also being an available and authentic friend instead of faking anything. This shift empowered me to get back to my business as a corporate emotional intelligence trainer and finally complete my PhD.

Unlocking Tool

Take a deep breath and stay with me for just a moment as I share a hard truth that often tugs at the heartstrings. When you die, very specific people will sit in the front two rows at your funeral, and almost everyone else will attend out of obligation. This is the reason the front rows are reserved for the people who truly feel the loss and absence of you from their lives. These people celebrated your successes and wins and mourned your challenges and setbacks. They loved your faults, appreciated your quirks, and were quick to forgive and defend you. They witnessed all the things that made you, you. These front two rows are evidence of your unique abilities and impact on this world.

These are the handful of people who will struggle to define your life in just a few words on your headstone. These last and final words are found above your name and are the meaning of your dash—that small line between your birth date and your death date.

Who are the three to five people who will find the final words to define what your dash means? Ask yourself who will attend your funeral due to the loss your absence makes in their life. When you think about your life through this lens, you see that your list of people is very few. The sooner you understand who these people are, the sooner you can define with whom you want to dedicate your time.

- Who would you invite for dinner if it was your last day on earth?
- Who would you sit and laugh with while sharing stories?
- Who would you kiss goodnight and make sure you embraced?

Those last moments filled with hugs, laughter with friends, parents, and children, and that final kiss are a compass on how you can design your life with consideration of those who care. Even if these people are not in your life now, you can define them. The more clearly you can identify who these people are, what they say, and how they make you feel, the rest of the decisions become so much easier. Don't waste time or energy on anyone who you do not see as part of your last twenty-four hours on earth.

If you dive deep into an audit of the people in your life and ask the question, "Will this person make a sacrifice for me?" this means they will give up something they value to provide for your needs.

There is a big difference between having someone stop what they are doing (especially if they are doing something they enjoy) to get you something you need and someone who is already doing it for themselves. For example, if I ask, "What can I do to serve and support you?" and you say, "Can you pick up my kid from school?" the level of sacrifice barely exists if your kids both go to the same school. In contrast, the sacrifice is greater if you are an empty nester who was at home relaxing with a good book.

Everyone else who shows up at your funeral comes out of obligation. They are participating based on their ego, meaning they are attending because they think they "should" be there and it is the right thing to do. It is about them and how it makes them look or feel to be there.

Anyone who has experienced loss can hear it when people say things like, "I am so sorry for your loss. They were so important to me too." Listen to how quickly the sentence went from about you to about them. Listen close when people speak, and hear if they are talking about you or if they switch and bring the conversation back to them. If it's always about them, they are the back row people at your funeral. It's about them and will always be about them.

There is a saying that if we die with five true friends in our lives, then we are living a wealthy life. This is the sign of having lived a meaningful life. These people understand the value you bring and feel the void when you are not around. They demonstrate this by sacrificing things they value to bring more to you. Their giving is an act that is not attached to wanting something or expecting something in return. When we know who these people are then we can pour into them instead of spending so much time in superficial relationships.

Chapter 4

It Starts with One Word

It starts with a countdown…10, 9, 8, 7, 6…all the way down until the clock strikes midnight and then millions of people around the world shout "Happy New Year!" Fireworks and noisemakers follow while celebratory couples and strangers kiss to commence the start of a new year filled with the hope of having their best year yet. It is a fresh start and an opportunity to look at the future with optimism. For some, it is a time to say goodbye to a particularly difficult year and to welcome the beginning of a new life chapter. The idea of a clean slate on January 1 is why more mental energy is expended on this day than any other day of the year on goals and resolutions on how to make or break a habit.

Some people create lists and lists of things they vow to do or NOT do in the new year. These are often a laundry list of unrealized dreams and resolutions regurgitated from previous years that automatically make it onto the list every year. How many times can we add the same fifteen pounds we want to lose, the same dead-end job we want to replace, or the same savings goal before we realize the list is not working? We often give more time, consideration, and planning to our grocery list for the week than to our resolutions. Why? Because we are one hundred percent convinced of the importance of food and nutrition in our lives. We don't need accountability, resources, or motivation to follow through on that task.

And then there are the vision board creators. They grab a poster board, a pile of magazines, glue, and often their closest friends to create a visual representation of what they want in the new year. The poster becomes the project. Sprinkled around the pictures of exotic vacations, jewelry, and embracing couples may be aspirational words like "happy", "best year ever", and "adventure". If they are lucky, the poster may make its way onto a home office bulletin board or closet, but most are discarded or never looked at again after they are designed and admired.

So, which one of these sounds most like you? New Year's resolution list maker or vision board creator? Or maybe you do not believe in any of it and are none of the above.

Turns out (and I bet you knew this was coming), neither of these exercises are effective because they are missing the critical component of deep thinking before these visual aids are created. The formula for success is 50 percent thinking, 25 percent planning, and 25 percent execution. If you have studied the greatest minds of our time, they all have one thing in common—they invest time in thinking. If you follow Warren Buffet or the habits of Steve Jobs or Elon Musk, a huge part of their days is dedicated to this practice. Most people are in fire drill mode and reaction mode, which is far from a practice of intentional thinking. Without this skill, your lists and vision boards are art projects, not life tools.

Statistically, very few resolutions or vision board pictures ever materialize or come to fruition. Most are abandoned and forgotten within weeks of claiming them as goals for the year. Although it feels like inspiring work to put pen to paper to create a list and build visual representations, *this way of approaching the things you think you want is wrong.* Your understanding of this statement will grow as we journey through this book, but for now, I want you to consider the following:

- The "why" behind each of your resolutions is more important than the item.
- What you *think* you want is not what you *really* want.
- The cost of getting what you "want" may be more than you are willing to give up.
- Nothing happens when goals are not aligned with feelings and actions.
- And finally, there is a better way to fulfilling your desire to improve your life and achieve your dreams through Designing Genius.

This book is the pre-work that connects you to your desired results. And not those generic and uninspired goals and resolutions of years past. No, I am talking about very intentional areas of focus that get to the core of who you are and what you really want from this life. This is not a superficial assignment. It is a way to work from the inside out, which is why you start with SELF.

Optimize YOU first, and then everything else you desire follows. Whether you are looking to improve your relationships—the ones you have and the ones you want—with more connection and communication, or if you want to build a strong presence within your personal or professional community network, or if you have goals around business and wealth-building, this journey always starts from within. Even if your biggest dream is a trip to Tahiti or buying a Land Rover, the process is the same.

Complete the Designing Genius exercises and witness the shift in how you view your life. Then put the plan into place and see how intentional actions create incremental results toward a life of fulfillment, happiness, and peace. The first step begins now, and it starts with determining your One Word for the year.

Knee Jerk Reactions

How do we find our One Word?

First, take a moment to imagine you are thrown into a crisis like your dog getting violently ill. Or if dogs aren't your thing, then picture your best friend calling you after finding out their partner is having an affair. Two entirely different situations, but both evoke a similar reaction from you based on where your mindset is rooted. When facing conflict, we start from one of two places. We either start with how we *feel* about the situation or what we want to *do* about the situation.

Neither one of these is right nor wrong because both sides of the infinity loop need to be completed. The only goal of the exercise is to establish how you would react first. If your dog starts getting sick then you may start by comforting your dog while getting emotional before wrapping it in a blanket, jumping in the car, and racing to the vet. Your initial reaction is facing the fear that your beloved dog is dying and life without them seems unbearable. Conversely, if you are more apt to immediately jump into action, then once the adrenaline wears off you may find yourself in tears and flooded with emotion. Your first response was more tactical like a first-aid checklist to wrap the dog, get them in the car, and call the vet.

What about the scenario where your friend's partner is cheating? Are you more likely to respond by asking, "How do you feel?" Or with something more tactical like, "What do you want to do?" Another way to think about this is by considering what reaction your friend expects from you when they call with this type of news. Would they expect you to be the friend who listens to them express their emotions and process their feelings? If so, you start with *feelings* first. If your friend is more inclined to call you because they do not know their next steps regarding actions, you should then take your starting place as rooted in *doing*.

To give you some context, the tables below list examples of *feeling* and *doing* words. One of those tables should make you feel more comfortable and seem more aligned to who you are as an individual. Pay close attention to the table that offers words that are the OPPOSITE of where you are rooted or feel comfortable. If you are more likely to lead with your feelings then the list of *doing* words is where you should focus.

Table 1: Being or Feeling Words

Vulnerability	Freedom	Choice	Belonging
Connection	Simplicity	Receiving	Focus
Seen	Trust	Stillness	Observation

Table 2: Doing or Action Words

Reflection	Money/Wealth	Integration	Independence
Movement	Expansion	Execution	Networking
Availability	Growth/Scale	Organization	Systems

Why is this important, and why should we care about our knee jerk reactions to a crisis or new situation? When choosing our One Word for the year, we need to choose the OPPOSITE of our natural tendency. Our word should feel uncomfortable and a bit scary because it is something we need to grow and develop in our life. If the word is "comfortable", then chances are that word is part of who we are today. We don't want to choose a word that represents an area in which we already excel. We are looking for growth and how we want our future selves to feel. The reason the word we choose has not been active in our life is that it triggers an emotion we are avoiding.

The *doing* is an external reaction, whereas the *being* or *feeling* is internal. Both things must grow in the infinity loop for maximum results. This is why we must do the work of choosing a word that is the opposite of our natural tendency. For many of us, this requires choosing a word that operates within our internal self.

Now you may be thinking that you don't want to be someone who starts with action or someone who gets all caught up in their feelings. That's okay because how you show up to these situations will not change. You are innately drawn to respond first with either feeling or doing. It is part of your core makeup. But in order to ultimately get what you want in life, you need to strengthen the opposite side of your natural tendencies.

When we stay in the area of our mind that is dominate, we maintain, but we do not grow. True growth happens in the opposite side from where we are dominant—we call this the shadow side. Your genius can often live in the shadow until you learn to bring it into the light. Growth is found in shadow work. This is why so many people stay STUCK. They only spend time on the side of their mind where they feel comfortable. This is where what they know is familiar. You will live in *"Groundhog Day"* forever if you only stay in what is known.

Think about it, how can you be an effective boss if you don't know how to connect? You may be an amazing visionary with a ton of marketable ideas but have a company full of dysfunction, disruption, and disgruntled employees because no one feels connected to you or the company. It does not mean you need to become soft or someone who doesn't take action. It only means you need to strengthen and develop within an area that does not come naturally to you. And if you recall from the beginning of the book, *the way you do one thing is the way you do everything.* So, if you are failing at connection at work then chances are this is happening on the home front too. And this is why we start with the One Word, so we can master and integrate a new skill into the most important areas of our lives.

Let's consider this from the angle of those who start with feelings first. You may be someone who is in touch with your emotions but need help putting action behind what you want. Maybe you feel stuck in your relationship, job, or even with your children. Life sometimes feels heavy, and you are not quite sure what your next step should be, so you do nothing. But what if you chose "movement" as your word? What if you vowed that for the next year you were going to intentionally focus on moving the most important areas of your life forward? And what if your Designing Genius plan did all the work for you to make sure it happened? If you can trust this process, you will find that your One Word will help you develop a new skill that you can continue to grow. These pages provide the steps needed to amplify all of you through either the *doing* or *being*. This is the pathway into discovering and becoming your highest and best self.

Your One Word

Let's start by identifying one overarching word for this game and for your perfectly designed year. More than anything else, what is the one thing you most want to feel? Notice that I did not ask you to identify what you want. If we come back to how our mindset impacts our outcome, then let's take a moment to define how we want life to feel. From there we will find the word that best aligns for what you want more of in your life.

As we have been discovering, your mind is a powerful tool. It can work with you (amplification) or against you (resistance). We want to build a safety net that makes it easier to spot when we are not moving in alignment with where we want to go. Let's choose a word that represents the strongest emotion you wish to build into your life plan.

Based on the last exercise where you identified whether you approach a new situation by *doing* or *feeling*, choose a word from the *opposite* table above. If you start by *doing* then your word will come from Table 1, and if you start with *feeling* then you want to choose a word from Table 2. Here are some examples to help you choose the right word for you.

For Those Who Start with *Doing*

If you are someone who likes to start with action, then your natural inclination may be to choose a word or theme for your year based on tactics and activity. We want you to push yourself to find the word that is on the OPPOSITE side of your brain and on the feeling side. If you feel drawn to words like "growth", "organization", or "systems", then dig deeper to locate the *feeling* word you would need to master to achieve your intended tactical outcome. Here are some examples of opposites:

- Growth can become Seen or Vulnerability
- Organization can become Receiving or Belonging
- Systems can become Connection, Learning, or Creating

For Those Who Start with *Feeling*

If you are someone who naturally *feels* before taking action, then it might feel uncomfortable to choose a word that is action orientated. We often unintentionally choose words or themes for our year in areas where we already excel because it feels comfortable. While this feels good, it does not give us the opportunity to stretch and grow into our best selves. It is about choosing your opposite, so you can strengthen that area in your life. Real growth always takes place in our shadow side. Based on the example above, we can select the *doing* word that lives on the other side of emotion:

- Seen can become Growth or Availability
- Belonging can become Organization or Networking
- Connection can become Systems or Independence

Testing Your Word

Before we fully commit to choosing our word, it is important to put it through a test. This word becomes the theme for the next four steps in this book, so we want to make sure we are choosing the right one. In the next chapter, we will be adding areas of focus where we want to direct most of our energy in the coming months. Our word dictates how we choose to show up for ourselves and others. Right now, this may seem a little difficult to understand, but as we start layering in your Five Areas of Focus, your Ingredients, and your Should and Should Nots you will see how your word becomes the umbrella that everything else lives under.

When it comes to our word—if we have chosen the right one—the reason it has not been active in our life is because the word triggers an emotion in us like fear, doubt, or uncertainty. This may be an emotion long buried within and rather than disturbing, healing, or understanding it, we have just left it alone. This resistance keeps us in a stagnant space, dulls our awareness, and limits our full potential.

For example, my word for the year is "vulnerability". There is nothing about this word that I like or want to confront. I prefer to stay tactical and active. Naturally, I am drawn to being in constant motion, providing solutions, and being a visionary within my business. The last thing I want to do is to lead my team and company from a place of uncertainty. Vulnerability to me always triggered uncertainty. As I have dug into finding my relationship with vulnerability—and in turn, a new part of myself—I am more confident and more certain living in my vulnerability. I started with the word "growth", which is an action word because I always begin on my tactical side. I knew that for me to grow, I needed to move to the *being* or *feeling* side (my opposite), which was vulnerability. As I have welcomed this word in, I found a new sense of self. This gifted me a new sixth sense of where to lead the company and a new way of building the team.

Crazy to think the way to your desired destination is through the opposite side of your knee jerk reactions. To fulfill my mission in life, which is to heal unintended pain, I must get close to my feelings and share them with others. Learning and practicing vulnerability will help me connect and empathize with others. It will create the type of relationships I need both personally and professionally to scale to where I want to go in life.

This is why we must test our word. If it already has a strong presence in our life, then we must look for a new word. Remember, we are Designing Genius. We are trying to bring our best and most aligned selves to life. Let's say that the word you are most drawn to is "growth", but you need to select a feeling word, so you choose the word "seen". The word "growth" may not feel intimidating, while the word "seen" triggers some fear because it is tied to emotions like:

- *Fear* of being seen
- *Fear* of not being good enough
- *Fear* of showing up authentically

Once you have chosen a word, put it through a test by answering the following questions. This will help you to determine if you have picked the right word to focus on for the year.

- Does my word feel slightly out of reach?
- What does my One Word mean to me?
- Why does this word make me uncomfortable?
- How will I know when this word is working in my life?
- What would I have more of in my life if this word was working?

We can use our word to constantly ask ourselves, "Am I showing up as my One Word?" It allows us to share our word with others, so they can challenge us to live up to it. For example, if you choose the word "connection" because you want to feel like you are part of something outside of yourself then you can prompt yourself to create connections with your neighbors by reaching out, connections at work by encouraging collaborations, and connecting with yourself to understand who you are in your soul.

You can build a support system that keeps you on track. If your partner knows that you desire to connect with friends, then they may encourage you to call a friend or accept an invitation. This also communicates to them the feeling you want to bring into your life that is currently missing. Unlike New Year's resolutions where we choose tactical goals like wanting to lose weight, your word is something people can help you achieve. The One Word you choose will create a feeling inside you when it is working. What you focus on, grows. If you are consistently focused on bringing this feeling to life, then it will grow.

Quick Fixes vs. Permanent Changes

You may be thinking that a quick New Year's resolution list or a vision board art project is sounding pretty good right about now. Wouldn't it be easier to rattle off a bunch of things that we want and then hope for the best? Yes and no. Yes, it is easier to transfer the same wishes and wants from last year, and yes, it is easier to choose words and aspirations in areas where we already excel. But…

- Where is the growth in your personal and professional life?
- Where is the achievement or results?
- Where is the evidence that what you are currently doing works?

Feel good solutions are not permanent fixes. They are only as good as the willpower behind them. Designing Genius will help you modify behaviors that are keeping you stuck. Think about my word of "vulnerability" for the year. Do you think that if I practice being vulnerable with my friends, family, colleagues, and partners for an entire year that it will permanently change my behavior and become a part of who I am? Of course, it will. However, if I had chosen a random word, theme, or resolution for my year, I'd be lucky if I achieved even a temporary result. Although aspirational, exercises like setting New Year's resolutions and creating vision boards do not have the thinking behind them for understanding their importance.

With Designing Genius, every single step has the intention of gaining better clarity around you and on how to live your best life. Once the process begins, it is woven into who you are. It simplifies your life because it becomes very clear what to prioritize and what to release. In the next chapter, you will choose your areas of focus and where you most want to spend and focus your energy on the coming year. This is when you really start to go narrow and deep into where you will apply your One Word and spend your time.

Susi's Story

Prior to meeting Amilya, Susi was feeling stuck in her life. She was letting her current environment dictate the future. Her thoughts and emotions on what she could not do were taking most of her energy and focus. Instead, she wanted to be focused on the amazing progress she had already made in her life and what she could do. The pain was excruciating, to the point that it literally paralyzed her. She was comparing herself to people in her industry for over twenty years. She spent a good year and a half in this frenzy. Read on to find out how Designing Genius tools have impacted Susi's life.

How did you try to fix the situation?
I have taken so many courses and talked to countless therapists. Therapists have not always clicked with me. For me, it was less helpful than speaking to my best friend.

What solution or tool did you use based on Designing Genius or something you heard from Amilya Antonetti?
Although it is not the easiest thing to do, I would say shadow work has been one of the tools that have changed my outlook and taken me to another level of mindset. This specific tool I find to be useful, but it requires you to go deeply inward, look at areas of you that you pretended not to see or forgot about, and intentionally make the behavior changes necessary to make a positive shift on hidden useless beliefs.

How long did it take for you to see a change or result?
In less than a month I was having lots of "aha" moments. Just shocking to feel, experience, and go through such a breakthrough at this speed. It has been fascinating. Proving me with solid clarity, a deep understanding of self, better time management, and tools and techniques to expand my business.

How is this situation for you today?
I am enjoying the process of becoming the best version of myself. I have finally learned to surrender, to let go, and trust. My business is flourishing, and I not only feel more successful, but I *am* more successful. I finally understood that being stuck is a natural part of life when there is a huge change coming up. Thanks to Designing Genius, I am redirecting my energy, my focus, and my time, guided by one of the most impactful and highly intellectual behaviorists in the world.

Unlocking Tool

Believe it or not, our minds are LAZY. When we experience traumatic events like the pandemic and the level of uncertainty, dealing with it is beyond most people's capacity. These Genius Games help guide you into deeper thinking to discover your current subconscious state. Where you are (Point A) is critical to understand. It is important to identify the markers and measurables your mind needs to move forward and grow. To search for your One Word, I want you to enter this game with this thought in mind.

You choose your One Word from your non-dominant state of thinking, referred to as shadow work. It is called this because it lives on the side of your mind you decide not to use or depend on. However, true growth is found in the shadow, in the unseen areas of our minds. As we discussed earlier, these two sides of the infinity loop reside in the *doing* and the *feeling*. Our life cannot scale without balancing them, which is why we choose a word that strengthens the opposite side. If your One Word is an internal feeling word, then the byproduct will be growth on the external side.

Genius Mind Bundle Exercise

Let's use a Mind Bundling game to dig deeper into how to choose the right word to get you to your desired result. Often you must journey through several words to get to your final destination. For example, if you choose a *doing* word like "growth", ask yourself, "What will I have to face in order to have growth?"

- You cannot have *growth* without *courage*.
- You cannot have *courage* without *vulnerability*.
- You cannot have *vulnerability* without *uncertainty*.
- You cannot have *uncertainty* without *bravery*.

This deeper thinking helps you select your One Word for the year. In my case, I knew I wanted to share my Designing Genius work with more people to create *growth* and *impact*. Both words are found on the tactical side of my brain—the *doing* side. In order for me to create greater success, I asked myself what emotion I must become to earn the opposite. For me, it is *vulnerability*. To be vulnerable to the criticism and judgment of others. The question I asked myself was, "What do I need to face in order to create a bigger impact or growth?"

Mind Bundle Two

- You cannot be *vulnerable* without being *seen*.
- You cannot be *seen* without being *authentic*.
- You cannot have *authenticity* without knowing your *truth (purpose)*.
- You cannot know your *purpose* without being *vulnerable*.

These Mind Bundling tools serve as a guide for your journey. Your shadow word may hit you in the gut and make you uncomfortable. If it doesn't, then you have the wrong word and need to dive deeper into the Mind Bundle exercise.

Chapter 5

Focusing on the Journey

Happily ever after is the ending to most fairy tales and children's book stories, but that is not based on reality. Many people spend their entire life chasing that ending and wonder why it never appears. This is because these stories are rooted in expectations. Expectations from Disney movies. Expectations from social media. Expectations from ads and commercials. Expectations about society's false perceptions of what love and romance are supposed to look and feel like. And all these stories are very damaging because you trade yourself for someone or something else.

What if instead of visualizing our story through someone or something else, we start pursuing a life story? Real life is much more beautiful and entertaining than any fictitious romance. Society has told men that women need grandiose gestures for them to be a hero. No. No. No. What people crave is daily acts of kindness performed consistently over time. These fairy tale stories create false expectations that neither side truly wants. Grandiose gestures can be a wonderful thing, but they are hollow if the day-to-day perfect moments are not present.

What if instead of expecting white knights, we became the hero of our own story?

Just think if we got to a place where we all started sharing more of our life stories and left these princess and white knight stories behind. A place where our journey, struggles, and life lessons were woven into history for the next generation of young girls and boys to hear. Instead of fairy tales where girls waited to be rescued and young men were the heroes, we created a path for each individual to be at one hundred percent from the very beginning.

This is where the life we design for ourselves comes into play. By doing the pre-work of first identifying what we want for ourselves, we can now match our needs, values, and desires with people who understand and respect our standards. Once this exercise is complete and we can say, "These are the components that make up my life," decisions become very easy. We can refer to our Designing Genius blueprint to ensure our relationships, jobs, inner circle, and sense of self are hitting the milestones from our list. Designing Genius is about bringing all the areas of your life that are most important to you into alignment. In this chapter, you will choose where you want to direct your focus for the coming year. This allows you to get very narrow and deep in a few key areas, so you can experience incremental progress as you move closer to creating your ultimate life story.

Your Five Areas of Focus

Your One Word set the theme for the board game, and now it is time to identify what areas of your life you want to focus on. Close your eyes and ask yourself, "What does my best life look like?" Don't worry about specifics, just let your mind wander and create a visual. Allow yourself to dream and build your absolute best life with no limitations. Don't let yourself fall into figuring out the "how". Only allow yourself to see and feel your most grand and ideal life.

What is the purpose of this exercise?

Think about this from the neuroscience lens of the "Red Car Theory" or the Baader-Meinhof phenomenon, otherwise known as frequency illusion. This theory says that if you have your heart set on a red car, all of a sudden, your brain sees nothing but red cars. It appears every person and their cousin is driving the car you want. Your subconscious mind starts looking for confirmation of this information, and you become more drawn to wanting it.

Just like the red car, the visual for our best life will start to show up everywhere if we do the work. In the same way, if someone chooses a red car, we want to be specific in where we direct our attention. Our brain cannot stay focused on too many things at a time, which is why we choose Five Areas of Focus (or puzzle pieces) to help us get to our best life vision. Once we get clear on these pieces, it is one hundred percent more likely the universe is going to bring those things into your life.

Let's return to our board game. As the theme, we have our word for the year. Now let's add the five big puzzle pieces that make up our best life. I will give you a head start by telling you that the first puzzle piece is YOU. To live a genius life, we must put ourselves front and center. There is no best life without taking care of yourself first by fulfilling your needs and desires for optimized living. Keep in mind that your Five Areas of Focus are totally customized to what is most important to you. Here is a list of some of the most common areas of focus to get you started:

- Partnership/Relationships/Friendship
- Business/Career
- Industry
- Community
- Wealth generation
- Creativity
- Adventure
- Specific learning (new language or skill)

The Five Areas of Focus you choose will feed into each day of your life moving forward. Focusing on small steps every day will compound over time and help you achieve your overall goals. As you can quickly see, this method is so much more effective than a vision board or resolutions list because everything we are doing is very intentional. It is not random. A typical vision board exercise is often with little thought and more dependent on which pictures we stumble upon from a magazine when choosing imagery. Nothing in Designing Genius is by accident.

Now that we have our five puzzle pieces, we want to add them to our One Word from the previous chapter. Let's pretend that our One Word for the year is "connection" and see how it fits in with our Five Areas of Focus puzzle pieces of "self", "partnerships", "career", "community", and "wealth generation":

- *Connection in Self:* I want to feel more connected to the things I enjoy doing like traveling, exercising, and cooking.
- *Connection in Partnerships:* I want to feel more connected to my spouse by having better communication and more quality time together.
- *Connection in Career:* I want to feel connected to my career and feel like what I am doing matters within my industry.
- *Connection in Community:* I want to feel connected to my neighbors by participating in more social events and interacting more.
- *Connection in Wealth Generation:* I want to feel connected to the way I have chosen to spend and save my money.

If you are following along by thinking about designing your life like a board game, then you would write your One Word at the top of your board as the game's theme. Then draw a horizontal line to represent where you are starting today, and then a finish line for where you'll land at the end of the year. Next, between these lines add the five puzzle pieces to your board. Leave plenty of room because we will add to this. For now, find one or two pictures that represent what each puzzle piece looks like in your life. *Connection* in partnership might include a picture from your wedding day when you and your spouse were madly in love, hopeful, and excited for the future. *Connection* in career may show a picture of someone working on a project that is aligned with their passion and genius. Keep in mind the pictures only need to make sense to you. Find the images that represent your ideal situation in each of your Five Areas of Focus.

Your Time Is Your Choice

Having Five Areas of Focus makes decision-making about how you spend your time and who you spend your time with easy. Building a life by design removes the guess work. This is what we'll discuss in the next chapter as we begin filling in the ingredients that make executing Designing Genius second nature. These ingredients are the first items you add to your calendar each week. Just like most financial experts advise you to pay yourself first, your ingredients based on self are the first things you put on your schedule.

You cannot pour from an empty cup or play a game without prioritizing yourself. If you are not healthy, rested, and recharged then none of your areas of focus receive the best you have to offer. Since we are Designing Genius and your best life, we need to create the time and environment for you to flourish. It is critical that you prioritize self-care on your calendar. Once you have made room for you on your calendar, you can start to fill in your other areas of focus.

Let's see how this plays out in real life with an example of an entrepreneur named Kara whose days have become a juggling act. She is building a new business, raising two kids, and trying to carve out quality time with her spouse. In addition, she sporadically exercises, volunteers in her community, and often gets pulled into school activities. Most days she is exhausted and operates in reaction mode. She feels like she's making little progress in any area of her life. The Designing Genius program is her opportunity to realign how she is living her life.

Seen is her word for the year, and she chooses the Five Areas of Focus that are most important to her in the new year. These are:

- *Self*: More self-care and time for herself
- *Partnership*: Dedicated time to grow her relationship with her spouse
- *Family*: Increased quality time with each of her children
- *Business*: Creating the foundational blocks to scale her company
- *Industry*: Gaining recognition within her niche

This exercise on its own gives Kara a lot of power and information. Based on this work, she has clarity around what will bring her happiness. It is not like the previous vision board exercises she's done with friends where random pictures and words have no meaning or action behind them. This gives her the confidence to say "yes" to the right opportunities and "no" or "not now" to those that don't fit within those areas. If the school PTA president asks her to lead a committee and it doesn't fit within these five areas, then the answer is "no". Think about it this way: Should a school committee take precedent over her marriage? Self-care? Or time from the business? Does serving on the committee get her closer to her goals?

Of course not. This may seem obvious, but we make decisions every day that move us farther away from our genius living goals. We justify it by telling ourselves, "It's just one hour" or "It's just one day a week", but when that hour takes away from having family dinners then the incremental cost of losing that time gets high. Eliminating the family connection creates a gap that you just filled with something that was never on your priority list. Multiply this with the countless other "asks" and tasks that make it into your day and you'll find yourself on a hamster wheel—one that may eventually cost you the things you value most.

The word "no" is a complete sentence when said with kindness and respect to the other person's question or request. It is an empowering and powerful word to use when necessary. We've all had days that started with the best intentions. Our schedule reflected our overall objectives and was organized to be super productive. We've also experienced that same day going totally off the rails with planned thirty-minute calls that last an hour, people asking for favors, and a child who remembers at the last minute they have a big project due the next day. The proposal you hoped to complete for a new client goes out the window and dinner consists of pizza delivery on a paper plate. These days will still happen, but as you get more intentional about your priorities and get better at saying "no", the occasional crisis will have less of an impact.

Having your Five Areas of Focus identified and your priorities in place makes it more natural to say "no" to the wrong opportunities or distractions because you already understand the trade you are making. With limited time in the day, how we spend our hours, minutes, and seconds comes down to choices. Just like in the example with Kara above, I don't think anyone would dispute that her marriage is more important than a school committee. Just like if a colleague asked her to create a new business product with them, she could tell them she appreciated the offer, but is focused on developing some foundational content for her company. The "no" is more of a "not now" due to timing. By being clear, confident, and direct with her answer, she handles that conversation with respect for herself and the other person.

But if you (or Kara) are not used to saying "no" or setting boundaries, it will take some adjustment. It might even feel a little strange at first, and that's perfectly normal. Here are some common concerns that come up when I am talking to clients about boundaries and time:

- I don't want to let anyone down, so I have a hard time saying "no."
- I hate saying "no" to something that is easy for me to do, but hard for someone else.
- My family already says I don't do enough for them.
- My best friend is always in crisis and keeps me on the phone for hours.
- I feel selfish taking time away from my kids to do things for myself.

Do any of these sound familiar? If so, you are not alone. The easiest conversation to have is the one before a problem arises.

Favors

Favors are expensive, and they are often what we say "yes" to when we should say "no." Favors take your time, energy, attention, and resources. Favors are a behavior that we learn at a very early age and are often confused with kindness, sharing, and reciprocity. Understanding the distinction is an important life skill we can teach ourselves and pass on to our children. Consider a teen during their development years and how easy it is to get caught up in wanting to fit in and please other people. This may require giving up a part of yourself or changing who you innately are. The stronger the sense of self that is built at this stage, the better we establish an identity we want as an adult. With peers, social media, and parental influences this can be a very confusing time, so identifying the Five Areas of Focus creates a more intentional game.

What if a teenager knew what made their highest and best self? What if they had five areas of their life to focus on that were identified by them? Think of the power of knowing how to best answer whenever a decision needs to be made.

If someone knows that to do one thing (a favor) they need to exchange something that was important to them, then they know the cost. For example, if an area of focus is getting into a prestigious college and their friends ask them to blow off studying for the SAT for a party, then they know what that party will cost them.

There's only so much time and energy in a day, so it comes down to choices. We can only pour the best version of ourselves into the things we value most. Everything else must get the leftovers. Understanding energy exchange can feel really empowering for someone who still has many constraints around what they can and cannot do because of their age. They can use it to make better choices regarding school activities, sports, academics, friends, relationships, work, and hobbies. If they pour into a romantic relationship, then they may have less time for friends. Play a competitive sport, and it may be hard to find time for a job. All these tie back into the areas of focus set by the teen.

When we do not create these guardrails on time then someone else may try to fill in the blanks. This can cause noise, confusion, and often disruptive activities. This is where peer pressure, bad decisions, and following the herd often comes into play.

These patterns follow us into adulthood where doing favors becomes second nature. We don't give a second thought to saying "yes" whenever someone asks for our time, energy, or resources. In the beginning, it may feel good to be that hero who saves the day. The "johnny on the spot" who people count on to step in and pick up the slack. As the "yes" to other people piles up and the "no" to yourself increases, eventually resentment kicks in. It no longer feels like a fair and equitable relationship because the giving is costing you something.

Bottom line, everything is an exchange of something and has a cost. Nothing is free. If you give time, attention, or of yourself, it is coming from or depleting from somewhere within you. If you are following Designing Genius, as you give of self, you also receive unto self. This is the infinity energy exchange. Without this infinity loop of giving and receiving, it is only a matter of time until you hit burnout. What you water consistently grows. That is why we pour first into our five areas daily. Never give the most important people you love your leftovers. Never give the most important areas of yourself the leftovers. Leftovers are for what remains after you watered what you are becoming in your life. In Chapter 7, we discuss how you create the guardrails around your time and interests as you develop the rules of the game so you can pour into your areas daily.

Scott's Story

Scott was facing a major life change prior to his introduction to Designing Genius. The program could not have come at a better time. After twenty-five years in corporate America, he decided to finish his career as an entrepreneur. The transition was much more challenging than he thought it was going to be. Read on to find out how Designing Genius tools have impacted Scott and helped him with this next chapter of his life.

How did you try to fix the situation?

I read A LOT of books. Mostly I was reading about entrepreneurship. But I sprinkled in some books on personal development. I was learning a lot and really enjoyed the content. But it was becoming clear to me that information and implementation are very different animals. Long story short, I was not implementing what I was learning. I simply went from one book to the next.

What solution or tool did you use based on Designing Genius or something you heard from Amilya Antonetti?
The Five Areas of Focus, the Ingredients, and the Should and Should Nots were eye openers. Ironically, the exercise allowed me to implement some of the concepts that I learned from reading all those books. In hindsight, the concepts of Designing Genius are not complicated—they are quite logical. But they are things that I simply wasn't doing. Just going through the process of identifying what areas of my life are most important to me, especially after a major life change, was the first and most important step for me. It gave me the clarity that Amilya talks about. Once I had the clarity, it became very clear what I should be focused on, and what things I should say "yes" to, and what things I should say "no" to.

How long did it take for you to see a change or result?
The change was immediate because my calendar became my trusted guide. I didn't just have a plan—I had a plan that energized me. I chose the areas of focus and was able to organize my day around doing the things that are most important to me. What could be better? Designing Genius is a no-brainer.

How is this situation for you today?
My wife says I am a different person (in a positive way). I have a completely different outlook on life. I still have obstacles and challenges, of course. But because I have a road map, it is much easier to get back on course when life happens. My only regret is that I was not exposed to Designing Genius in my twenties or thirties. My kids won't have that regret!

Unlocking Tool

Most people have not made the connection of how closely the association is between time and money. What we know about human behavior is *the way you do one thing is how you do everything*. So, if you do not have a healthy relationship with time, you most likely do not have a healthy relationship with money. In this game, you are developing the awareness that time is one of your greatest resources, just like money. How you identify and relate to time and its value will have a similar pattern or belief to your relationship with money and the other things you value.

$86,400 Investment Fund

This game teaches you to invest your time like you would invest in an opportunity. The opportunities in this game are the five areas you have identified as your areas of focus. These are the things that are the current deal breakers in your life as to how you spend your time. This game creates awareness and helps you develop boundaries around your time based on what is important to you.

Gameplay:
1. You begin the exercise by getting $86,400 to spend any way you want with one caveat: the money must be spent in a 24-hour period, or it will be lost.
2. Set a timer for 10 to 15 minutes and create a list of how you will spend the money.
3. After the timer goes off and your list is made, it is time to group your investments by category. Did your investments align with your Five Areas of Focus?

Consider why you chose to spend the money the way you did. Now that you are looking at the categories, are there any items you forgot or would change? Do your investments reflect your areas of focus?

The amount of $86,400 was chosen intentionally because it is the same number of seconds we have in a day. See if your actual calendar and schedule match how you said you would spend the investment. Are you as intentional with your time as you are when choosing how to spend the money? The goal is to bring you awareness, so you spend time on things that are as important to you as when you believed the 86,400 equated to dollars. The more you develop the awareness of the value of something, the more you stand in the position to protect or defend it.

Chapter 6

Your Key Ingredients

Ask twenty people about their ideal morning routine and you will get twenty different answers. The list may include coffee, exercise, and breakfast. Some will drink their coffee black, while others like flavored creamers or particular blends. Exercise may mean a bike ride on a Peloton, a run in the park, or a rigorous weight-lifting class. And as far as breakfast is concerned there are food, location, and dining partner options. These nuances and preferences are sprinkled throughout our days to create a recipe for success. When we miss doing these things or don't prioritize them, we lose the momentum that having these things in our life gives us.

In this chapter, we are identifying what needs to be present in your life so you can show up as your highest and best self. These are what we call "Ingredients". We want them to become the non-negotiables on your calendar. With Designing Genius everything is customized for you and by you. There's no one-size-fits-all when it comes to building and transforming your life. While many people reading this book will choose the same One Word and Five Areas of Focus, it is unlikely they will have the exact same ingredients list.

Your Five Areas of Focus create the balance in your personal and professional well-being. Similar to the five points of a star, each has its own lane but remains balanced regardless of which direction you turn it. In a perfect world, we live in the center of the star. Our One Word is integrated into each of our Five Areas of Focus and is the common thread bringing our life into ebb and flow of a genius life. The ingredients are what give meaning to each of those five points. Without them, there is no definition of what makes a successful self, business, partnership, or any of the other areas we have chosen to focus on.

Your Ingredients for Self

Now things are going to get really fun because we are going to add to our Five Areas of Focus by selecting the ingredients required to become our highest and best selves. These are your ingredients with no right or wrong answers. Let's put this exercise in the context of a family dinner where everyone decides they want pizza. Everyone in the family absolutely loves pizza, but each of you has a different idea of what toppings make up the best version of an ideal pizza pie. One of you likes meat lovers, while another is a cheese lover or a fan of veggies.

So, let's translate this into our five puzzle pieces starting with the most important area of focus, which is "self". What ingredients make the highest and best you? What must happen daily for you to feel like your absolute best? Consider what you need as part of your morning and evening routines; practices that help you to feel positive, calm, and energized. Think about your ingredient list as it relates to your overarching One Word from Chapter 4.

For example, if your word is "vulnerability" then an ingredient that helps you feel positive about vulnerability may include practicing meditation in your morning routine. Meditation provides the grounding and stability you need to show up vulnerable. This demonstrates how the One Word and ingredient flow in the same direction. The ingredients must move with your word. For the word "vulnerability", ingredients that are defensive or protective will not work as it is impossible to go in two directions at the same time.

Once you list out your ingredients to be your highest and best self, ask yourself if you have flow with your word. Here's some prompts to help you get started on your ingredients list:

- Do you flourish with reading? Yoga? Walks in nature? Stretching? Weight training? Dog cuddles? A morning kiss?
- Do you flourish with healthy food and plenty of water?
- Do you flourish with a bath and glass of wine?
- Do you flourish when you are seen and valued in your career by knowing your work makes an impact?

To discover what these ingredients mean to you, think through these questions using your senses. What would you hear when you wake up in the morning? Birds chirping, waves crashing, or your partner telling you they love you? What would you see? Maybe it is flowers, the gym, or a warm cup of coffee. And lastly, what do you feel? Is it energized, creative, or calm? The more you have clarity on the ingredients, the easier it is to design your genius life.

Based on your answers to these questions, your first area of focus for self may include the ingredients: nature walks, quiet time, gym membership, healthy food, and relaxing baths. When it comes to our board game, these ingredients are the proof that we are on the right path. Consider the game Chutes & Ladders. When you climb a ladder, you are traveling in the right direction. Land on a chute and you move backward. The ingredients you choose are the ladders taking you toward the life you want to lead. Use them as a compass to guide you to optimized living.

When your chosen ingredients are present in your life, you are connecting to the highest version of you. This goes back to why this exercise is much more impactful than resolutions where the only milestone or proof is if you achieve the goal. Living a life by design allows us to produce the evidence and to communicate to those important people in our life how they can encourage us every day.

When we surround ourselves with people who intentionally help us execute the ingredients we need to become our best self, we build a network that is supportive and caring. We align both our priority of self and our internal energy with the people who want us to succeed. This creates the internal and external energy to move in the same direction. The truer the intent, the more the frequency or the energy we give off attracts other frequencies that are vibrating with this same "care" and "intention." The beauty of this alignment is that anything that does not have the same positive energy will create a glaring awareness of being out of sync. The more we harness our mind with this knowledge, the easier it is to move away from the energy, people, and things that do not have our best interests in mind.

This work begins to unlock the reality that what we desire, what brings us joy, and what needs to occur to make us feel better about our life is not so far out of reach. When we identify these ingredients for ourselves, those around us are then empowered with this information. They have a new understanding on how to connect, love, and help to care for you in a way that has meaning and value for everyone.

These simple tools can quickly impact a disappointing, stressful, or frustrating day and transform your mind back into a space of gratitude and love. When you feel like others understand you and can provide the things that bring joy, you become more connected with the feeling of belonging. Living a life where you are seen, heard, and have a sense of belonging is a powerful place to be.

If your best-self ingredients require a long bath at the end of your day, your partner may put the kids to bed, so you can get your much needed self-care. Or if getting outside in nature is one of your ingredients, a walk with the dog may recharge you and put you in a better frame of mind. The beauty is in the simplicity that Designing Genius brings into our lives and those around us as we begin creating the rules for our game.

Your Ingredients for Partnerships

After you have started identifying the ingredients that create your optimal self, it is time to start filling in the ingredients for your other areas of focus. For many people, that second area of focus is either partnerships or relationships. Not everyone defines these words the same way, so it's important for you to establish your definition of the word to bring clarity and focus to your life.

Always keep in mind that you cannot have what you don't define. This is why identifying what it is you want and defining what you mean—specifically, with as much detail as you can—helps bring what you really want. If you do not define it, then you will get sloppy versions of what that word means. This is why I encourage you to create your minimum standards for everything. Knowing what the minimum requirement is for each of these five areas gives you the power to communicate to others that they must demonstrate these minimums in order to get the gift of who you are. This is so important. I cannot stress this enough. If you do not know what you want and why those specific things are important to you then you are guessing and hoping through life, and so are the people around you.

Please don't "hope" your way through life. Invest the time to design and live an intentional life. The definition of success is when you live the life you intend with the people who matter most to you. That is the home run. It is not the material objects, the random followers on social media, or the vanity titles in your chosen profession. It is the people you choose to be part of your genius life who become your most treasured objects. As you can see from the following questions, the word "partnerships" can take on many meanings depending on what you are needing most in your life right now.

- Do you desire a romantic partnership? Or to grow and "next level" your current one?
- Do you desire a professional partnership? Or to create more synergy in your current situation?
- Do you desire to be an amazing parent? A better friend, sibling, child, or member of the community?

By asking yourself the right questions you can get closer to creating your ingredient list.

Keep in mind that you are choosing items that are relevant to your situation right now. Next year, some of these things will be different. If you are single and desire a partnership, then it is one hundred percent easier to locate it and grow it when you do this exercise and build your partnership area of focus. Depending on what type of partnership you want to strengthen at this time, your ingredients list may look like:

- **Romantic Relationship:** loyalty, intimacy, affirmations, physical touch, quality time, acts of service, gifts, getaways
- **Professional Partnership:** teamwork, collaboration, trust, accountability, personal development, equitable investment, return on time, money, and resources into what has value and meaning to you
- **Parent Relationship:** trust, laughter, one-on-one time, quality conversations, outings, pool days, game nights, movies, mentorship, transferring your knowledge into the next generation for greater impact
- **Friendship:** confidentiality, unconditional support, fun, travel, coffee dates, exploration, and adventure

As you can see, the ingredients are often a combination of internal qualities and external features. For example, you may seek a partner who is loyal and trustworthy, and someone who wants to travel the world with you too. These key ingredients are your ideal representation of this area of focus. You may not have them in your life currently but know what you are building toward your future best life.

Now that you have a better grasp as to how you can dive deeper into defining your areas of focus with ingredients, challenge yourself to think beyond your typical "go to" answers. Stretch yourself into new territory by identifying ingredients you may have thought were out of reach. This is where growth and scaling come into play and enhances your personal and professional life. As you bring more of these ingredients into your life, you will no longer settle for anything less. This re-setting outside of your comfort zone creates a new baseline.

When It All Comes Together

Let's look at a sample board game from a corporate executive named Tony who has spent the last ten years doing the same things both personally and professionally. His One Word for the year is "movement". This word scares him because he has a safe and secure job and a predictable personal life. He is relatively satisfied but feels something is missing. Tony's Five Areas of Focus are self, partnership, career, wealth generation, and community. When he closes his eyes, he can form a really clear picture of what he wishes he had in each of these areas of his life, but he can't imagine it is possible.

This is where his ingredients come into play because they provide the prompts that will get him to where he wants to go. If he stays accountable to them, it is impossible for his life not to feel more aligned with how he wants to live. Tony identifies the following ingredients for each of his areas of focus:

- *Self*: hiking, healthy low-cholesterol diet, eight hours sleep, reading, and painting
- *Partnership*: date nights, travel, laughter, and intimacy
- *Career*: innovation, challenges, collaboration, and networking
- *Wealth Generation*: real estate, new venture investments, and life insurance
- *Community*: non-profit involvement, neighborhood barbeques, and coaching son's baseball team

Tony finds pictures to represent each one of these ingredients and adds them to his life board. Looking at his list, do you think Tony's life will dramatically improve if he incorporates them into his life? Do you think he will *feel* more movement in each area?

With all this information, how much easier is it for him to complete those ingredients and share them with the important people within his areas of focus? His Designing Genius life board will become a cheat sheet for Tony and his family to demonstrate he is living a life by design. His family can develop their relationship with Tony and be confident they are giving him exactly what he wishes to receive.

Make It Visual

After you have chosen the Ingredients for each of your Five Areas of Focus, it is time to add the visual imagery. Find pictures that represent each of these ingredients and place them next to the appropriate puzzle piece. Remember, these are the evidence you are doing the work. The pictures only need to make sense to you. This is your Designing Genius life board.

Your Designing Genius game can be created with a posterboard like a vision board, digitally on Pinterest or in Canva, or anywhere you desire. The format is not important, but the location needs to be visible. Your Designing Genius game is not a "set it and forget it" exercise. Your One Word, Five Areas of Focus, Ingredients, and rules of the game are your daily guide to living. Your life plan will influence how you schedule your days and weeks, how you engage with others, and impact where you spend your money, energy, and resources. Life becomes what we practice repeatedly. This is why creating rituals and routines are critical to success and living your best life. No one lives their best life by accident. It's always done when you decide to make it intentional.

Plus, the best news is that the more you invest in building these genius tools, the more people in your life will lean in to help you achieve your goals. You are literally handing them a cheat sheet to your designed happiness. This is the kind of cheating we welcome in life. Share with others how you want to be loved and watch the world love all over you. The images you choose should answer the following questions as to how and why they contribute to your areas of focus:

- How does this picture represent my highest and best self?
- Why does this ingredient help me and my life?
- What does this ingredient represent to me?
- Why do I want or need this?
- How does this contribute to growth within my One Word?

Let's unravel this last question a bit, so we can see how our One Word and Ingredients work together. Using our example of Tony and his word *movement,* consider what it looks like with the ingredients he chose for "self". *Movement* in activities like hiking, diet, and painting means he must become active in order to find success. Instead of wishing and wanting to do these things, he must execute them. He must move outside of his internal feelings about these ingredients and strengthen his external self to create balance in his infinity loop, or better yet "ebb and flow" with the laws of nature. When you move, your environment moves too. Nothing grows while stagnant, so if you desire movement in your life, you must be in motion to receive this energy of movement.

See how this works? You put your self-care desire for movement out into the world energetically, and you will then receive movement back. This is part of what is meant when you hear, "You get back what you put out into the world." It starts within you. The more you understand and make the connection between what you want, how it makes you feel, and the way you show up, the more you will embody what you want. You become love and attract more love. You become movement and attract more movement. What you seek in the world must live within you to gain and receive it.

Everything that "is" or exists in the world moves closer or farther away from its source. If you want movement, you must become the source of movement from within you. Everything about you must drive from this one overarching word by begging the question, "How does this thought, this belief, this action move me closer to my best self?" If what you are thinking does not move you then the thought is not serving you. Any time you have a thought that makes you feel stuck, cancel that thought, and create a new thought that aligns with what you intend, which in this example is "movement".

This applies to any One Word you choose. If your word is "belong", any thought that does not bring about a sense of belonging is a thought that needs to be canceled and swapped out for a new thought, even if you must temporarily force a new thought. Eventually, the new thoughts will replace the old ones. Here is how this works:

One Word:
Belong

Negative Thought:
These people have been working together forever. I will never feel like I'm part of the group.

Awareness:
This is a stuck thought that I will never belong.

New thought:
I am canceling that thought and am calling forward the imagery of me sitting at a restaurant with this group, laughing.
We go out every Friday to kick off the weekend and celebrate a successful week at work.

The new thought has a lot of details to counteract the negative and misaligned thoughts that we want to replace. From a behavior standpoint, when we want to move away from toxic or non-serving thoughts, we need to cancel and create a new thought stream with lots of details. These details and adjectives cause our mind to pay attention. Think of it as daydreaming or day thinking. Others like to call it visualization. What I want you to take away is learning the PRACTICE to cancel unaligned thoughts and replace them with intentional thoughts that move you toward your goal.

Now that we have discussed how to design a life that identifies what we want, we need to simplify the path to get there. Designing it was the first step. The next step creates the clarity of who we are as a player of our game and who we want sitting next to us at the table. It is not enough to create the plan; we also need the strategy to execute it.

Dami's Story

After a brain injury, Dami had to adjust to an ADHD and ASD diagnosis. She had started to put some systems in place to help her become the best version of herself by journaling and meditating when she found Amilya, but she was also grieving. Decades of walking around in the dark had caused years of lost opportunities. Read on to find out how Designing Genius tools have impacted Dami's life.

What have you tried in the past that has not worked?

Hearing Amilya on Clubhouse sharing parts of her story and the behavioral tools she used to thrive, and her "tough love with a hug" style of calling out limiting behaviors, brought into stark focus that I'd been living out learned patterns that were not serving me. With growing awareness, my default character mode had become playing small, overly accommodating others, and failing to put myself first. I realized I was raised to go against my instincts. In a transitional moment in my life, I approached the solutions presented by making the effort to drop the things unworthy of me and getting into alignment with myself.

Somewhere between trying to heal my "wounded child" and rewrite the "the old Dami" narrative, I found something was gone. The brain injury which had unearthed my neurodiversity also relieved me. I felt validated to accept a life where bad organization, depression, a warped perception of time, and impulsivity weren't just character flaws. Yet accepting neurodiversity as my new story felt like a setback. It would exclude me from my dreams.

What solution or tool did you use based on Designing Genius or something you heard from Amilya Antonetti?
Amilya talked me through one of her behavioral tools. I'm going to call it P.O.S: Pain – Opportunity – Suffer. The creativity fueling my award-winning filmmaking was nowhere to be found. Knowing a better version of myself once existed, my internal monologue had nothing but insults for me. As a result, I was making myself small and unworthy of my voice, which used to shine. Amilya helped me see a new perspective using P.O.S. Her message is to let PAIN be your greatest asset and use it as an OPPORTUNITY to grow. By using that pain unapologetically to create impact, I can prevent someone else from losing out on the ability to learn from my experience…and avoid suffering. I was exposed to a new possibility! I can be the champion for others and not just the victim of my circumstance.

Whilst struggling to let go of perfectionism, I embraced and immersed myself in Amilya's Designing Genius program and became really aware of lots of my old patterns steering me off course. My behaviors around "Asking Big" and making myself the priority needed to be ignited with new momentum. The first step to writing a new narrative for my life was asking someone who has experienced rough terrain for directions.

How long did it take for you to see a change or result?
Amilya has been there and has created a road map of behavioral tools to help you get on route to your destination quicker. By working with her, I've noticed the ripple effect in my professional life. With plans to impact the mental wellness of one billion people worldwide, I created Filmmakers Therapy Couch, a platform "amplifying stories that heal and transform".

It launched with a web series that spotlighted storytelling's visionary creative leaders, who aligned with my mission. From Issa Rae to Dawn Porter, filmmaking rock stars supported me by sitting on my proverbial 'therapy couch' to share their 'quick tip therapy' on how to flex your creative muscle. I was producing, filming, directing, hosting, and editing the show myself and hadn't even thought to ask anyone for help. By the time I was finally burnt out, and entering into motherhood, it was too late.

Amilya helped me reactivate my genius with a new approach to my behaviors. She practices what she preaches. I've added structure to my life, unleashed the power of my voice to Ask Big, and learned to get out of my own way. Am I there yet? I'm certainly headed in the right direction, and the growth of Filmmakers Therapy Couch is evidence of this.

How is this situation for you today?
I need help, and I have started asking for it. I am impacted now with a clarity of thought where I can trust my inner compass not to sabotage my purpose. I'm designing a life much bigger than my inner taunting voices imagined. These tools have provided a gateway to self-discovery. The human behavior awareness gained in the Designing Genius program aids in self-discovery so we can all show up like the champions we were meant to be.

Unlocking Tool

I often say, "You don't know what you don't know, and be careful who you allow to fill in the blanks." The following game helps you organize and grade the level of importance of your "knowledge exchange." This means that if you ask your mom if you are attractive, she will undoubtedly say "yes". However, her knowledge or input on the topic is biased and therefore less "important" in the formula.

Part of sustainable success is learning to put the right level of importance on the information you are receiving. This is where so many relationships and businesses fail. You are asking for information from people who either:

- have not demonstrated success on the topic OR
- their success conflicts with the desired outcome

This game will help you better categorize what type of knowledge exists within your circle of influence and the credibility of the information you will receive. I like to ask myself the question, "Do they have the receipts?" In other words, is there proof of knowledge and expertise?

The Knowledge Exchange Game
Here is a quick game that you can play with the five to ten people with whom you spend the most amount of time. Remember, we already know that you become the average of who you spend the most time with, so let's decode who you are becoming. Complete one of these questionnaires for each individual on your list.

Gameplay:
1. Write the name of the person.
2. What is their overarching genius? For example: financial, technical, organizational, healthy lifestyle, etc.
3. Are they making money with their genius? This is important to know as it gives you information on what can be implemented into your life and what information needs further details.

4. What is the highest level they have hit with their genius (this determines the degree to which you should utilize the information)?
   a. Applied knowledge or not applied knowledge
   b. Making a living
   c. Other people pay them for this genius
   d. They have sold and exited a company with this knowledge

Now that you have identified what areas of knowledge your circle of influence offers, let's intentionally begin to align your area of focus from Chapter 5 with this information. Based on your Five Areas of Focus, add the name of the person who has genius in that area or some type of knowledge that can help you move closer to your goal. As you learn about rules of the game in the next chapter, think about the following Should and Should Nots you can create to help you with your circle of influence.

- I should intentionally identify and check in regularly with the people who demonstrate the successful outcome I am looking to achieve.
- I should keep the name and contact information of the person who has mastered a key ingredient in the Notes section of my time blocks within my calendar.
- I should not allow opinions to influence my goals and the actions I need to take toward my goals. Advice is worth a dime, and experience is worth millions. I only take real-time experience into account in my decision-making.

Play this game and adjust several times a year as you grow and develop within your areas of focus. At the same time, realize your area of genius is something that someone else is hoping to develop, so be sure to reciprocate in the knowledge exchange.

Chapter 7

Rules of the Game

All games worth playing come with instruction manuals. They explain how the game works when it comes to winning and losing. Along the way, players can move forward, be rewarded, and complete a journey. Or they can receive penalties and never make it to the end. Every consequence in a game has a pre-determined outcome that is understood amongst the players. This is what rules do. They bring the players mentally together to establish a baseline of understanding. The understanding of the rules allows each player to come to a sense of "neutral". Once the rules are understood, then all movement from there is based on the decisions made by the individual player. This is where the individual demonstrates their skills, autonomy, and choices to compete fairly in their quest to win.

We are conditioned from an early age to know that everything in life has rules and structure. Without them people feel lost. When a person doesn't feel like they know what they are doing, where they fit in, and why they are participating, it creates an uncomfortable feeling of uncertainty and exclusion. They don't understand how they belong to the game or the other players. Rules, or what I refer to as "boundaries and guidelines" create the parameters of:

- What am I doing?
- What is expected of me?
- What role do I play in it?

These rules provide clarity and a sense of security for people. Many research studies show how much happier and productive people feel with rules and structure. When we provide people with our rules (minimum standards) we help guide them on how to have a relationship with us. These same rules provide us with the checks and balances we need to confirm we are living up to our own standards. When we become accountable to ourselves, we build confidence, worthiness, and connection. The first person we must build safety and security with is ourselves. If we do not know what rules we need for our own highest and best self, it is impossible to give or receive these things from others.

Just like board games, our lives cannot operate without rules. If we do not establish what we will or will not accept for our life, then no one (including ourselves) knows how to play the game. Everyone is set up for failure from the very beginning.

All our life experiences, including the pain and challenges, are what got us to where we are today. They are what makes us who we are today and have delivered some of our greatest gifts, so we don't want to deny those events. But now, we can make more informed choices. We do this by answering the question: "What is and is not serving me in my life right now?"

We don't want to change anything about who we are at our core. We are worthy just as we are. The purpose for examining ourselves is to nurture those areas we want to develop to their fullest. Heal the areas that need care and let go of the aspects of ourselves that once served us but are no longer needed. Hold that part of you with huge gratitude for how it served you until today and gently come to peace that this part of you is no longer needed and can be released. We want to always honor who we were, who we are in this moment, and who we are becoming. Think of it as the law of being. As we grow into the best version of ourselves, we remove behaviors that no longer serve us and replace them with something positive that fills that gap.

We often move into the "doing" too quickly. What if we paused a minute, took a deep breath, and instead examined the risk versus reward of our decisions. Any one thing we choose to do is going to vibrate to something we must choose to give up or can no longer do in order to make space for this new thing. We cannot grow and develop anything if we do not first make the space, the room, for this growing to take place. If we have our day crammed with activities from sunup to sundown, life will likely feel like the movie *Groundhog Day*. Without space to think and process, we cannot make the room required for growth. It comes with understanding the ripple effect caused by our decisions and what we tell the universe we want. Each decision impacts the next. This is the awareness that comes with establishing the rules for our game.

As discussed in this book, our mind is a powerful tool. It can work with us to amplify the positive or against us to create the resistance. By selecting one main overarching feeling we want to focus on, we can choose those things that serve us and eliminate or reduce those items that no longer help us be our best. This principle not only applies to our behaviors, but the behaviors of those around us.

Our word for the year provides us with a quick check and balance to make "yes" and "no" decisions. For example, if you remember Tony from the previous chapter, his word is "movement." Any "ask" of his time, energy, effort, or resources should be tested against his One Word. It should positively answer the question: "Will this activity bring me closer to feeling movement? Or is it triggering a feeling of being still?" When we intentionally build our game to help us direct our energy and resources to where we are going, we are designing a blueprint that ensures success.

The rules help him create the rules for HIS game. This is a selfless move on his part because once people understand what those rules are, they can choose whether they do or do not want to play. This sets up the proper expectations on both sides. Without these rules, everyone is sitting around the same board game but playing by a different set of standards. Now everyone is confused, unsuccessful, and feels unfulfilled by the experience. When there are no rules, we create unsuccessful energy and relationships without meaning. The experience is awful as people stumble and fall while trying to figure out what is going on. No one feels like they are getting what they need from the relationship. This happens often in meetings, partnerships, and during family time where no one knows what they should be doing. Boundaries or rules set up any situation for more intentional success because everyone is on the same page with clear expectations. It's a process based on creation, communication, agreement, and then execution in order for them to work.

Establishing Your Rules

These rules (or boundaries if you better identify with that word), which I call the "Should and Should Nots" of our lives are the checks and balances we glue into our lives to measure how we are feeling. The Should and Should Nots share YOUR rules of the game with the people in your inner circle, whether it be family members, friends, colleagues, or romantic partnerships. If the rules don't work for that person, then it's okay, but they are at least clear on the role they will have in your game.

The easiest way to start creating your rules or "Should and Should Nots" list is to return to your Five Areas of Focus and your Ingredients. We have already identified those puzzle pieces as the most important areas of your game, so it only makes sense to create boundaries that protect them in your life.

Let's return to our friend Tony and help him create the rules for his game. If you recall, his One Word is "movement" and his Five Areas of Focus are self, partnership, career, wealth building, and community. Based on each of these, he can start by creating two to four rules for each area. The point of this exercise is to protect those areas of our life that we have identified as important and the ingredients they require. Here's how Tony might do this:

Self: hiking, healthy low-cholesterol diet, eight hours of sleep, reading, and painting

Should
- *I should spend thirty minutes a day doing something creative.*
- *I should go to bed by 10 pm and wake up refreshed at 5 am.*

Should Not
- *I should not start working until I've taken care of my mental, physical, spiritual, and higher self needs.*
- *I should not let other people's fires become my fires.*

Partnership: date nights, travel, laughter, and intimacy

Should
- *I should schedule a special date night every week.*
- *I should have more vulnerable conversations with my wife.*

Should Not
- *I should not let my work keep me from taking time off to travel with my wife.*
- *I should not take my wife for granted.*

Career: innovation, challenges, collaboration, and networking

Should
- *I should pursue a more challenging position within my company.*
- *I should pitch my creative ideas to my work team.*

Should Not
- *I should not avoid attending networking and work events.*
- *I should not keep quiet when I have a better solution.*

Wealth Building: real estate, new venture investments, and life insurance

Should
- *I should purchase life insurance to protect my family.*
- *I should learn more about real estate and how to earn passive income.*

Should Not
- *I should not let a lot of money sit in a savings account at my bank.*
- *I should not loan money to family, but instead say "no" or offer it as a gift.*

Community: non-profit involvement, neighborhood barbeques, and coaching son's baseball team

Should
- *I should build my legacy around being charitable to my favorite non-profit.*

- *I should use my organization skills to put together some fun weekend get togethers.*

Should Not
- *I should not refuse invitations to neighborhood gatherings.*
- *I should not prioritize work over my son's activities.*

Based on what we know about Tony and his desire for movement, do you think these game rules will help him reach his goals? Will they effectively communicate to those around him what his wishes, wants, and needs are from other people?

Your "Why" Unlocks Your Power

As you build your list of rules, it is important to uncover your *why*. Taking the additional step into understanding why you chose each rule or boundary gifts you deep insight into who you are and what you value. For example, one of my Should Nots is "I should not be yelling." If I have to raise my voice or get loud for someone to hear me or pay attention to what I am sharing, then it is an immediate red flag that the relationship is not healthy. I do not like who I am when I yell. I have removed people from my life that trigger this behavior. There is no reason I ever have to raise my voice. I have highly effective communication tools and can discuss anything and everything in a calm and controlled manner. My "why" for not yelling is that it was part of my childhood that did not work for me. I was in a yelling household, so loud voices throw me back into a space where I am triggered with feeling unsafe and vulnerable to abuse.

People in my inner circle understand that yelling is not just an inconvenience to me. Yelling causes me damage and harm due to the triggers I associate with it. If someone knows this about me and still chooses to yell as a form of communication, it is a major red flag that this person does not care about me. Do you see how unpacking the "why" behind each of the rules can show you how to connect the dots as to how you became the person you are today? It allows those who care about you to understand why your requests for this structure contribute to you being your highest and best self. They will want to help you honor this request and more importantly, remind you when you are not enforcing the rules.

Self

Many people start to feel panic at the mere thought of designing the rules or boundaries for their lives. As much as they crave the authenticity and the truest pathway to success by asking for what they need and want, they freeze in the execution. Why? Because of fear. Fear of rejection, drama, or conflict. You may feel that you are being asked to create rules in an environment that has been running on autopilot, when in fact, rules did exist, but they weren't created by you. The fear around rules really exists because people don't want to communicate them. This is where the true anxiety grows. They fear the emotional rollercoaster of what they perceive as potential for confrontation or conflict.

When you are conditioned or in the habit of being one way with people, the thought of changing may bring fear of rejection right to the surface. Most people are afraid they will not get the buy-in from others that they want in order to make these changes. They are fearful of ridicule, being made fun of, or the scrutiny that comes when someone speaks up for the first time. I want you to stop and explore these feelings of fear and ask yourself, "What is the worst thing that could happen to me?" I want you to play out this scenario in multiple ways and decode the answer. Is the real fear a lack of buy-in to your new boundary from someone else? Are you waiting for permission before you make changes in your life? Buy-in gives power to the person you are wanting or seeking it from. This means you are waiting for someone else to stand up and take action to provide a healthier designed life for you.

I think we both know that this means you will be waiting forever. If you do not design your life with your rules and boundaries, then you are living someone else's life. Anytime we live someone else's life, we live with an emptiness that starts and grows from within. We can never truly fulfill what the other person is looking for because it is not part of our innate being, so we fail at the image they want of us. We then fail on both fronts. We are not living up to the expectations others are placing upon us, and we are not living up to the person we want to be.

Once we step into designing our life, the people who care about us and care about knowing who we are at our core will step up too as we design new standards and boundaries. If we want more, we must create the framework and rules to receive more. I promise you it is never as scary as we think. It is always surprising to witness how many people welcome the guidance on how to best pour into you in a more meaningful way for you. Think about the reverse. Don't you want to give the people you love and care about exactly what they need from you? Don't you want to support them on their life's journey toward living their best and most authentic life?

Remember, people are glued to the story that they need to believe. So many of us need to believe that if we speak our truth regarding rules and boundaries that we will end up alone. This story in our head builds and grows to the extent that it stops us from reaching for the very things we want the most. We don't speak up. We shrink who we are and allow others to chip away at our very essence.

Let's decode this for a minute. The things we are the most afraid to ask for are the things that we want and need the most. If we are afraid to speak up to the people who claim to love and care about us, then what does that say about our relationship? If they disappear when we set a boundary, then maybe their role in our life is not equitable or respected. Contorting who we are and sacrificing what little time we have left to pour into someone who is not willing to meet us at the halfway mark is a recipe for unhappiness. Both sides of the relationship need to give and receive value. It cannot be one-sided if we want it to thrive.

Defending a relationship that does not respect your rules and boundaries is full of resistance and negative energy. Nothing good can grow there. A beautiful thing happens when you start pruning and releasing these relationships that are not serving you. Those who can and want to will come forward. Life blossoms without the toxicity. It is like removing the weeds that are choking the flowers. Once they disappear, the flowers bloom bigger and more boldly than ever before.

Some of your rules are meant just for you. Casual and new acquaintances may be unaware of them like, "I should not be kept waiting for a coffee date" or "I should not start working until I've completed my morning routine." These are to set healthy boundaries for yourself, so you are protecting your non-negotiables. For many busy people who often put themselves last in their personal and professional life, this is a good place to create rules around self-care and communication boundaries.

Then you have close people like your partner and close friends who will respect and help uphold your rules, so you can deepen your relationships with them and yourself. It is important to share your rules with them, so they know where you have chosen to draw the line in certain areas of your life. As your support system, not only will they want to help you stay accountable to your own rules, but they will want to follow them too. This open dialogue will likely encourage them to share their own rules with you. This awareness and clarity help each side realize they have both been unintentionally violating each other's rules because they didn't know the rules or what game they were playing. This is how strong relationships get stronger.

Time-Blocking Your Shoulds

An easy way to reinforce your "shoulds" and protect your time is to use time-blocking. Oftentimes, our boundaries are created because outside influences of people or things take us further away from something we want. Blocking time off on our calendar to do the items on our ingredients list gets us closer to achieving the goals we have set through Designing Genius. It removes the distractions. For example, if your best friend often calls you when you are trying to write a book then your Designing Genius plan for writing a book may look like:

> **Area of Focus:** Career
> **Ingredients:** Write a book
> **Should/Should Nots:** *I should schedule one hour every day to work on my book. I should not answer the phone, emails, or texts when I am working on my book.*

As you can see, this is very specific. This person knows they need to time-block an hour a day and turn on the do not disturb feature on their computer and phone so they can stay aligned with their area of focus. If you recall from earlier in this chapter, Tony knew exactly how he wanted to protect his time in order to reach his goals for the year.

A great place to start when developing your Should and Should Nots (especially if you find yourself stuck) is by tracking all your activities over the course of three workdays. For three workdays, write down every single thing you do, from returning emails, attending meetings, and working on projects, to the smallest of jobs like using the copy machine, answering a text, or picking up groceries. Let's assume that based on the work you've done so far in this book time is an issue for you, and there are many things you want to accomplish, but you're still wondering how to fit it all in. Now, let's audit your task list for the last three days by identifying:

- How many times was I interrupted throughout the day with other people's issues?
- How many tasks did I complete that can be done more efficiently? For example, getting groceries delivered instead of going to the store.
- What projects or items did I work on that energized me?
- What teammates or collaborations got me excited?
- What tasks did I find draining?

Based on this list, you can now create your Should and Should Nots to protect your time and energy. These will allow you to prioritize your time, so you can schedule your high energy tasks first. Many people like to create boundaries around their work time where family and friends can only text them in case of an emergency, so that someone else's personal life doesn't wreak havoc on their workday. This is the beauty of Designing Genius—it is one hundred percent customizable by and for you.

Tariko's Story

Tariko had been through several failed relationships. He was in a place where he couldn't trust anyone after being deceived and not recognizing it for himself. Read on to find out how Designing Genius tools helped Tariko identify and communicate what creates trust in his relationships and life.

What have you tried in the past that has not worked?
I've tried everything from counseling to talking to a therapist, pastors, friends, and family.

What solution or tool did you use based on Designing Genius or something you heard from Amilya Antonetti?

In one conversation with Amilya, she validated and encouraged a simple process that eliminated so much cloudiness. She told me that trust was very important to me. I needed to be okay with communicating with someone about how they can win it with me. She encouraged me to tell a person exactly what I needed, and it would give them the opportunity to build trust. She also said when anything changes it is my responsibility to re-communicate what I need.

How long did it take for you to see a change or result?
This changed my whole mindset and gave me the empowerment to ask for exactly what I needed in each day-to-day scenario. I took her advice and consistently communicate. It has shifted all my relationships. Originally, I was focused more on my romantic relationships, but I started to implement it across the board, and it shifted all the relationships around me. It helped me notice

that I expected others to know how to serve my genius, but I hadn't given them a blueprint to execute. Once I was able to identify what I needed in each area, I was able to provide what I needed. This provided clarity and precision for people around me to hit the mark.

How is this situation for you today?
Amilya has given me a trust that has eyes, and I now walk without blindness. I'm able to "see it" in all my relationships. I've learned that when there was no trust within self to properly communicate, then I was not giving myself what I needed nor was I providing to others what the "Should and Should Nots" were. It truly is Designing Genius!

Unlocking Tool

Many relationships have different power dynamics or operate on different playing fields. This happens between adults and youths, bosses and employees, and often in relationships. Taking a moment to observe someone else's vantage point and then opening the door for communication is the first step toward making everyone feel comfortable and safe in the relationship.

Ace of Hearts

This game requires two people and two decks of playing cards. Organize one deck in order, in the correct suits, all facing the same direction. The other deck is all mixed up with some cards facing forward and some backward, making it much harder to find the Ace of Hearts.

If you are trying to drive home a teaching moment to someone who shows up as a control freak or dictator, then you want to hand them the unorganized deck proactively. By the end of the exercise, you want them to understand how other people feel when they believe the cards are stacked against them, living in a dictator-type or overly controlled environment. If this exercise is used in a group setting for general awareness, then neither participant is aware of the organizational differences between the two decks.

Gameplay:
1. Give one deck of cards to each person.
2. Ask them to race each other to find the Ace of Hearts.
3. The winner finds the Ace of Hearts first.
4. They have fun racing through the cards, but the person with the mixed deck usually gets frustrated or complains that it is not fair. This is amusing when the adult is the person losing, and the child is the person winning. The person with the mixed deck needs to have the "aha" to understand why they feel the way they feel and how this may relate to other situations within their relationship with the other player.

The person with the perceived power must be aware that they have the upper hand in that relationship. Acting like things are equal when they are not is insulting and hurtful to the other person. In the case of a parent and child, or manager and employee, some of the power dynamics are necessary, but so is open and honest communication essential for building a relationship based on respect.

In other circumstances, where the playing field is not neutral, but should be addressed through Diversity, Equity, and Inclusion (DEI) initiatives and workplace programs, this exercise aims to recognize and acknowledge that not everyone starts with the same deck of cards. In relationships, the person who earns the most money sometimes has the most power over spending and decision-making, or the other partner feels and acts like they do. Awareness and acknowledgment are the keys to opening the door to deeper discussions in any of these situations.

Chapter 8

Relationship Rule Starters

"And they lived happily ever after" is the end to many fairytale romances, but that is not the reality of life. Not once did any of those stories put any activity behind their words. Yes, there was a knight or prince. Yes, he swept the beautiful girl off her feet. And yes, they rode off into the sunset. This is beautiful and magical for fiction and cartoons, but reality requires that we put in the work so that our friendships, partnerships, and romantic relationships can find and sustain success. If not, we get carried away in the beginning with excitement until the newness fades, and we are left with real problems and issues.

The beauty of Designing Genius is that you do the work independent of anyone else, so your rules and boundaries are already established before relationships begin. You are not chasing a problem with a new solution. You set the tone and rules from the very beginning and invite the other person to share their rules too. Everyone begins in a powerful and successful position because they know what the other person needs and expects.

Friendships and Business Partnerships

Consider this: There's a difference between setting a conversation up for success and throwing your emotional or life frustrations onto your friend's side. If I call a friend after work and say, "You will never believe what happened to me today. All I need you to do is listen because I'm going to rant for just a minute, so I can get it off my chest." This is much different than me charging into the call full of emotion and saying, "Today has been a total disaster. My boss is such a jerk. Can you believe he yelled at me after throwing that last-minute project on me?"

Do you see the difference? In the first example, I'm letting my friend know that their only responsibility is to listen. I don't want them to try to fix it. And by starting the conversation with "I just need you to listen" they understand I'm not asking for an opinion or solution. This sets them up for success because they are not trying to solve a problem that does not exist.

In the second scenario, I'm setting my friend up for failure. They cannot fix my problem, nor do they need to absorb all my emotional energy. Oftentimes someone can vent, get something off their chest, and then feel calm. There's no reason for both people to get worked up or overly involved in an often-unsolvable scenario. Those six simple words—"I just need you to listen"—are so powerful in all our relationships.

When establishing our rules of the game we can reverse this by stating, "I will not allow others to throw their problems onto my side." This may be important for the person who deals with a lot of family drama or has friendships where they are the go-to person when people are having difficulty with their spouse, children, or at work. You can be having a perfectly great day and then with just one phone call someone else's fire can become your fire and ruin your energy and momentum. These rules may be difficult to enforce at first, but you can start by saying, "I am sorry you are having a challenging day. Can I call you back when I have an opportunity to focus all my attention on what you are expressing? I can hear your need and want to give you my best." By putting parameters around when you are and are not available, you are letting people know that you care but cannot drop everything whenever someone calls. At the same time, this should bring you into awareness of how you manage your own problems and interactions with people and their time.

Business partnerships sometimes have an extra layer of stress because both a personal and professional relationship may exist. There's no right or wrong way to set rules for this relationship, but both parties must agree about how to handle off hours and whether business is discussed. Creating these Should and Should Nots and sharing them can reduce friction, disagreements, and misunderstandings between people. One person may want to work ahead on the weekend, so they can stop working early a few days a week to attend their daughter's softball game, whereas their partner likes to totally unplug on Saturday and Sunday and then hit it hard during the week. Having an open dialogue around your rules keeps the line of communication open, lets people know what is important to you, and builds trust between people.

When I work with people who have two distinct roles like being someone's life partner and also their business partner, or they are a doctor and also a business owner, we immediately define each role and assign a visual cue on when they are a husband/wife and when they are the business partner. We give each role a different name, visual, and environment. For example:

- I use a pet name when I am connecting personally and intimately.
- No business is discussed in the bedroom, kitchen, or bonding living area.
- Either person can ask to speak only about business or personal issues without switching between the two roles.

This sets the foundation for building each relationship and not confusing the intimate relationship with the business. By tapping the subconscious with sensory cues that say this is our business relationship and this is our intimate one, both relationships can grow to the fullest potential. Without boundaries, there is confusion.

Dating

Dating is a tricky situation. We crave partnership and compatibility yet need guidelines on how to interact as we increase intimacy. This is often when we try to put our best foot forward and be on our best behavior. Known as the honeymoon phase, this is when our attention and focus is at its highest. If we use these communication tools during this phase, we dramatically increase the sustainability and depth of the relationship. When we feel seen, heard, and valued for who we truly are and are equally embraced for the rules of our game, we are building on a strong and authentic foundation.

We create conflict if what needs to be said does not get expressed. If we do not set boundaries or speak up when we are bothered by a particular situation, the tension will build until one person explodes or walks away. Partners sharing rules (Should and Should Nots) gives both people an opportunity to show up as their most authentic self and play the game. Without these instructions everyone is guessing and hoping they get it right. Or even worse, hoping they can bend and change the person into who they want them to be. Neither option creates a healthy or peaceful relationship.

Having these non-negotiables clearly articulated between partners sets the standards of what each person will and will not tolerate and how we expect to be treated. If you are with the right person, and they see the value of having you in their life, then there is no length that person will not go to maintain the relationship. If a partner behaves in a way that makes you feel wanted, welcomed, valued, and respected, it is because they want you, value you, and respect you. It is that simple. The way we are treated is a clear indication of where we stand in their life. Every once in a while, do a regular check-in and ask yourself, "How does this person make me feel? Do I feel valued? Do I feel like I am a priority? Do I feel cared for?" Knowing how someone makes you feel tells you way more about them than you realize.

Words are designed to support actions, not replace them. It is important to pay more attention to how people treat us and not be misled by what they say or promise. This empowers us to choose more wisely. The biggest heartaches come from words that never had any action attached to them. Here are some simple ones that are quite common:

- "I'm sorry."
- "I'll call you back."
- "I'll think about it."
- "I promise I'll quit…"
- "It won't happen again."

Empty words are an indicator of a behavior where someone likes or loves the "idea" of you but does not really value or accept who you are. If you allow yourself to fall in love with the idea of things, life will always feel empty. Broken promises and hollow words are a violation of trust. This is why Designing Genius is about "being" and "doing" and threading it throughout our lives. We set our rules before any violations occur, so we are proactively establishing our minimum viable standards before the game begins.

For example, a person may have a fifteen-minute rule where that is the longest they will wait for someone to show up for a dinner date without communication. The key is to stick to the rule. The first time you enforce it is uncomfortable, but it sets the tone for the relationship. Without the rules, they will disrespect you over and over again while you are still in the honeymoon stage. The responsibility you have to yourself during this "magical thinking" period is to stay present and not attach yourself to the other person too soon. The rules you set will attract the type of relationships that are compatible for you and repel those that are not.

Those same red flags that show up during the honeymoon phase are the same issues that will eventually end the relationship. If they are always late and time is important for you then there is an incompatibility issue between the two of you in this area. In the beginning, the two of you don't know each other and are not attached, so it is easier to hold boundaries. You are demonstrating self-care and self-love by holding true to your rules and standards and doing someone else a favor because the relationship is ultimately going to end how it began anyway.

We cannot love someone more than we love ourselves, and it is not fair to sacrifice our life for someone else's. Whether it is a new relationship or one that has already started, we can set these rules and start by putting new practices into place. If not, we are more committed to our partner's happiness than our own, and that is abuse. You are abusing yourself by removing happiness from your life.

Rules are what protect us from energy vampires. When we enforce our rules and boundaries, like with the fifteen-minute rule example, our energy elevates our vibration and frequency because we choose the life we desire. It is taking a step forward and absorbing none of the negative. These moments provide an energy boost versus the drain that comes when we do not stick to our personal guidelines.

One rule that should be shared between partners centers around the word "all". We've become great at delivering "some" of the information while omitting the other pieces because we don't want to hurt someone's feelings. Trying to save someone by filtering information is disrespectful to our partners by placing them in an unhealthy parent/child relationship. When we give someone all the elements then they can decide how to react based on their own feelings, experiences, and emotions.

Knowing how to deliver all the information is sometimes one piece of the puzzle, whereas an apology may be the second step. A "should" that needs to be on everyone's list is: *I should receive and give proper apologies.* Learning how to offer an apology will strengthen relationships, while disingenuous ones will destroy them. The only goal is for the person wronged to feel seen, heard, valued, and recognized.

What is an apology? It is an awareness and acknowledgment of a mishap. The worst thing we can do is pretend or act like what we did is not a big deal. "I am sorry" is not an apology. A true apology includes four steps:

1. Awareness: *I know I am late.*
2. Full responsibility: *I kept you waiting. Waiting is frustrating.*
3. What you could have done differently: *I could have left my house earlier, so you weren't kept waiting.*
4. Future plan: *Here's what I am going to do differently next time: I am going to leave work twenty minutes earlier and text you that I am on my way. Does that work for you?*
5. Sincere apology: *I am sincerely sorry. I know it was a waste of your time to get here early, when your time could have been spent more productively then it was while waiting on me.*

The way a person you are dating does or does not respond to your rules and boundaries is an indication of how the relationship will progress if you choose to make it permanent or long-term. If they do not respect what is important to you then they will either feel the rule does not apply to them or will totally ignore it. They will never offer a proper apology because they will not feel one is truly warranted. Instead, it will be a delivery of words without action. Establishing your rules of the game allows you to identify your standards and rules before you enter your honeymoon phase with someone, so you can make the best decisions for you and your future.

Getting really clear on WHY you are dating is a major component to having success. I firmly believe that if you do not know why you are dating then you should not be participating or using other people to figure it out. Spend time discovering yourself and identifying what you are looking for from dating. This sets you and others up for a much more enjoyable and healthy experience. If you meet someone who cannot clearly articulate what they are looking to gain from dating, then this is a red flag. You can never give or share anything that has not been defined.

Marriage

Long-term relationships and successful marriages are malleable like clay. They have the flexibility to stretch, grow, bend, and even break before coming back together again. This is necessary because the people we are when we enter a relationship are not the same people we are ten, twenty, or thirty years later. We change and evolve. What we want for ourselves, our partnerships, and from life will ebb and flow from year to year. If we do not take the time to build that new life together and instead stay stuck in the old idea of each other and the dreams from decades ago then the relationship falters. The key to creating long-term partnerships is creating the "third entity".

What I Want + What You Want

=

What WE Want (the Third Entity)

It is no wonder that so many people wake up and discover that after years and years being together, they are lying next to a complete stranger. It is because one person is still operating based on the twenty-year-old version of their relationship while the other person is operating as their fifty-year-old self. One mindset is in yesterday (that no longer exists) and the other is in a future that also does not exist. The more you can identify who you were, who you are now, and who you are becoming, the closer to authenticity you become. These are the ingredients that your third entity is built upon. The third entity is development planning when we begin integrating who we are today into what we want for ourselves and together as a couple. It can be an exciting conversation to re-imagine the future, intimacy, communication, and lifestyle.

It is perfectly natural for our wants and needs to change and evolve over time. Often, when we come into a relationship we bring with us baggage from our childhood, experiences from other partners, and preconceived notions about what life for us is supposed to be. As we get older and exposed to new people and ideas, we begin to see other possibilities.

As we get into relationships it is important to unwind and heal what transcended during our inner child development, so we can detach from the things that are no longer serving us. Our partners need to be aware of the shadow work we are doing, so they can help us identify the inner child behaviors that are still showing up in our adult relationships and running rampant. This creates awareness and understanding about the behavior.

Shadow work is where genius and brilliance exist. This is where our greatest gifts live. It is a blessing and a curse because our greatest strength is also our greatest weakness. The shadow work is what we learned as survival skills during development. This shows up particularly in people who had a difficult or complicated childhood. The *shadow*, a false sense of self, was created in order to survive the environment.

A lot of times in partnerships, we learn to tolerate or argue with someone's behavior, but we do not know what is going on below the surface. We do not know the root or the basis for the resistance energy. This energy can cause a disconnect and negatively impact intimacy. But once we understand the behavior and the desire to move away from it, we can work together on a solution. Then it becomes about pulling out the old behavior and replanting a behavior that works better. We then practice it over and over again. Identification is the key. We call this start, stop, and swap.

For example, if someone experienced a toxic relationship or was told they were not deserving of love and attention, they may have difficulty asking for help or receiving someone's time. They don't want to feel like a bother. Anything of value like time, money, or help will be a struggle because they don't feel worthy. The underlying belief system is, *I'm not good enough.*

Imagine how this shows up in a partnership where one person struggles alone and the other one feels helpless because they do not know what is happening. This is disrespectful to the partner who has not been trusted with this information because now one partner is making decisions for the other as if they are not a capable adult who can choose whether to help. This creates a parent-child relationship that does not work. In a healthy adult relationship, people need the ability to express their needs. It is then up to their partner to express whether they can or cannot help and in what capacity.

Understanding the dynamic of how a behavior trait such as not feeling comfortable asking for help will allow both people to come together and lean into each other's perspective in a supportive manner. The awareness allows the practice to take place in a safe environment. It can start small by asking someone for five minutes of their time to help out with something like making dinner. Eventually, that old behavior of not wanting to bother someone will detach and a healthy new pattern will attach to reinforce the feeling of being worthy of someone's time.

Giving and receiving is an infinity loop. They are connected. Pouring into people and loving them feels good and brings so much joy. If we deny someone else of that feeling because we cannot "receive" what they are "giving" then we are robbing them of the same joy and experience. We are actually hurting them by not leaning in and learning to receive.

A truly nurtured partnership has depth that comes from consistently watering the relationship so it can flourish and grow. What you do not consistently nurture and water dies. We want to constantly pour into it and allow our partner to pour into us. Wherever we direct our focus will grow, so we do not want to "feed" the most important person in our life with leftovers. This is why we honor each other by holding the space to express our gratitude on a daily basis.

Protecting vs. Defending

Rules are meant to create predictability and consistency, which is why it is so important to create boundaries in your life. All of us were raised differently, and some generational traditions that were once popular and even considered chivalrous are now seen as offensive. The Should and Should Nots remove assumptions because they are based on where you are today and what is important to you right now.

Do you remember how in Chapter 1 we discussed that our behavior is either protecting or defending something in our lives? This applies to the people we love and care about and how we show up for them. Our brain is wired to defend ourselves against threats. Many men were taught to defend the women in their lives, whether it was their sister, mother, friend, or partner. This is what is often referred to as "chivalry" in fairy tales where the defenseless and helpless maiden waits for the hero or knight to appear and defend her honor or rescue her from evil.

When someone is defensive, they are often protecting their ego. It is based on a combination of their beliefs, feelings, and personality. They want to believe they are a good, intelligent, or likable person, and they want others to think the same. They want to justify their decisions, the things they've done, or even who they are as a person. Underneath this defensive behavior is ego, and underneath the ego is fear. The fear is that maybe they are wrong. The biggest issue with getting defensive is that once triggered, you are totally closed off to learning, connection, and growth. All those options disappear because you become committed to staying in the same place.

So, what can you do when you come up against someone who is defensive?

Start by stating your reality: "Hey, I am feeling some tension from you. Would you like to stop talking about this topic or is there something that I can do differently? My intention is to connect with you, and it feels like I am off to the wrong start." By addressing it and calling it out, everyone has an opportunity to restart.

Then listen. Don't try to fill the pause. Wait for their response.

If the conversation is not going anywhere or if either party needs a break, then that may be the best course of action in the moment. If the conversation feels strained or charged, then start by changing the environment. Any time there is tension in a conversation it is always best for both parties to be sitting down. This will reduce the tension and neutralize any physical size advantage one party may have over the other. It is also acceptable to suggest discussing the situation at a different time when everyone has had a chance to think and calm down.

The key to having success with these behavior modification tools is if you are going to take a pause in the conversation then you can't leave it open ended. This creates major anxiety for at least one of the parties involved. It is similar to when someone says they need to talk to you and then leaves you hanging. Your brain spins out of control. A healthy and responsible communication flow is to ask for time to think and state when you will be able to participate in the conversation next, so you can collect your thoughts. Here are a few examples:

- Can you give me an hour to think on this?
- Can we discuss this after dinner? I think I will be able to show up better after I eat.
- Can we discuss this in the morning before we both start our day?

The same level of uncertainty occurs when we ask for someone's time and attention, so we want to be more specific. For example, "Do you have some time to chat about something that's been on my mind? I want to get your thoughts on a decision I am making about my health." When you relieve someone from the stress of having to figure out what it is you want to talk about, they do not bring that "charged" energy into the conversation.

So often when I work with partners, a big part of the misalignment comes from how they set up the conversations. If you care about someone, you want to give them the basics of what you want to discuss. This needs to be set from your lens, which means the conversation needs to be about you and not them. For example, if you are upset about the shoes piled up by the front door, you can say, "I am feeling some anxiety about my environment and would like to run some ideas by you and get your thoughts on a solution that could work for us regarding the house." During the conversation, you can suggest an area where only your stuff is located. This allows you to demonstrate what a supportive and nurturing environment looks like to you. From there, you can expand the area slowly as you set up the rest of the home for success. The key in all these examples is to have positive and open communication between the two partners. If you don't start on neutral ground, the conversation is already doomed to fail.

When working with a couple who was having communication issues, I observed how the two of them held conversations. He was six foot one and she was five foot five. In one of the first exercises we did, I had her stand on a chair and look down at him when they were speaking. This allowed him to see how it felt to be in the non-dominant position. Size can certainly impact the outcome in the situation, which is why it is best to be sitting while having crucial conversations.

When someone defends another, they subconsciously tell that person that they are not capable of defending themself. This is what happened when Will Smith jumped onstage during the 2022 Oscars and slapped Chris Rock for telling a joke about his wife Jada Pinkett Smith. One of the first public comments Jada made was that she did not ask her husband to defend her and that she does not need that in a husband. Although Will Smith had good intentions, he overlooked the energy of his defensive actions.

Whereas protective energy is different. This is when you are energetically saying that "I am worthy and valuable." It is proactive versus reactive. In a work setting, being protective means that the company creates a community of inclusivity and respect. As a parent, we place our children in age-appropriate safe environments. And in relationships, we protect our partners by reinforcing and respecting their boundaries. As you start to think of the words defending and protecting, you can see how the push and pull energy feels different. The rules of the game really help us to lock this into place, so that we can remove ourselves from the position of defending or the one being defended.

Mario's Story

Mario faced the constant struggle of knowing he was meant for more. He knew he was not an accident on this planet, and that we all have a place of belonging. Not only himself, but his generation struggles with this feeling of not having a purpose. Being told you're not good enough, not feeling understood, or feeling unique was difficult. Read on to find out how Designing Genius helped Mario start focusing on the areas of his life that truly mattered to him right now.

What have you tried in the past that has not worked?
I have tried bottling up emotions and problems, thinking they would disappear. I was distracting myself with meaningless consumption of games, food, and anything that didn't acknowledge the problem. Pouring so much into working without acknowledging, whether that work aligns with where I want to go or if it feels right, left me most of the time feeling empty rather than feeling full and alive.

What solution or tool did you use based on Designing Genius or something you heard from Amilya Antonetti?
The most helpful tools were the Five Areas of Focus and the Should and Should Nots. I had not taken the time to figure out

what is most important to me. Everything can't be equally important, and if I have too many areas of focus, I can't truly focus on the ones that will leave me feeling aligned and full of energy. The Should and Should Nots were helpful to put into words. I felt but didn't always acknowledge the areas of life I should be doing within that focus and where I should not compromise.

How long did it take for you to see a change or result?
Once I took the time to go through the course and write everything down, I was able to start living with it more intentionally. You have to do the work with anything we choose to do, or else we won't see any results. I feel like I was able to find change almost immediately because I was not aware of the areas that are important to me and the tools to implement them. Every day may not be perfect, but once you have the list and tools in front of you, your baseline awareness gets better and better each moment of the day.

How is this situation for you today?
My situation today is all about living more intentionally. It means that if something doesn't lead toward my goals or leaves me feeling good inside, I don't give it my attention. It's important to know your blind spots, and while you can do a lot of internal work yourself, having a coach or a program to help pull more out of you to be more aware of what's going on has proven to be so impactful in my daily living and my future.

Unlocking Tool

Success with establishing rules of the game comes from the implementation. Some of these you can do yourself, but many require you to effectively communicate them to others. The way you share those boundaries and rules dramatically impacts how they are received and the eventual outcome. The art of communication is to master both the listening and the receiving of information. This unlocking tool will amplify your knowledge of pace and fact finding and will help you practice listening and identifying what you learned.

Pass the Baton Game

Oftentimes people with communication issues fail to take the time to hear what the other person is actually saying. Listening is at the core of effective conversations, and we cannot do this if we are in a state of debate. Sometimes we need to slow down the pace, so neither person is waiting for the other to finish just so they can make their point. This ping-pong style of banter is where disagreements, misunderstandings, hurt feelings, and unresolved conflicts grow.

This activity allows both parties to hear what the other person is saying before responding. It also allows people of different skill sets and ages to learn how to communicate effectively. Whether it is parent-to-child or partner-to-partner practicing, this exercise will give you a tool to respect the boundary of "listen before you speak".

How to Play

This activity requires a facilitator who can properly set and hold the boundary of listening in place. A physical object is going to be passed between participants, so a baton, flashlight, pencil, or any other object can be utilized for this game. The pause while passing the object creates awareness to both people about how they are thinking about what they are going to say next instead of listening. For those people who have a reputation for stepping on other people's words and interrupting, this is the game for them.

Gameplay:
1. Begin this game by handing one of the participants an object (baton, flashlight, pencil).
2. Explain that the only person allowed to speak is the person with the object.
3. Ask the participant with the object to choose a real or fictitious topic of discussion (where someone would often step in with advice or an opinion). The facilitator prompts a participant to say to the other person, "I want to talk to you about xyz, and I just want you to listen."
4. The participant with the object talks about their topic and then passes the object to the other person.
5. This person must now practice listening without giving advice or interjecting their own thoughts and ideas.

Both parties will learn a lot from this exercise because oftentimes we ask for advice and then do not like what we are given. This triggers the defensive mode where people then claim they did not want interference. On the flip side, we like to fix problems. It is difficult to bite our tongue and not speak up when we have preconceived ideas about something. Many times, those ideas are wrong because we jumped to a conclusion without listening to get the full scope or harness the ideas the person has already vetted and why. We bump up against unwanted and unsolicited thoughts when in truth, it is more that we do not know how to ask for what we need.

During arguments things can escalate very quickly when the need to be right outweighs anything else. This is such a common habit that people do not even realize how much they are committed to being right. When you start conversations without a clear foundation, you make it very hard for either party to know how to listen. When you cut off listening, you remove the knowledge you actually are seeking to understand, which is an alternative perspective. Mastering the ability to "knowledge exchange" is a gamechanger in any type of success. He who can access and apply knowledge usually wins. There is nothing worse than an empty conversation with no substance. It feels like a waste of time and in many cases a total energy sucker. Slowing down the tempo by passing an object gives both parties the time to absorb what the other person is saying, so the conversation has engagement and depth.

Chapter 9

Living the Perfect Day

Think back to when you were a kid and were used to hearing the word "no" from your parents when you asked for something at the store. Or when you were a teenager and asked for a later curfew, wanted to dye your hair, or asked for a car. Chances are you got used to hearing the word "no" a lot during those years. And because of that, you may have spent a lot of time thinking about what you would do when you got older that would make your life amazing or perfect like:

- When I get older, I'll buy a Corvette.
- When I get older, I'll stay out late every night.
- When I get older, I'll live in a big fancy house.
- When I get older, I'll do whatever I want. Nobody is going to tell me what to do.
- When I get older, I won't work in a boring and miserable job like my parents.

And then, we get older. And we may or may not do those things from the list above, or maybe we just stick pictures of those things on a vision board. Either way, none of those things make us feel at peace. In most cases if you ask someone what their perfect day would be, they have no clue. Even those who make vision boards have not taken a deep dive behind those pictures to uncover "why" and "what" those pictures represent, let alone if they equate to their perfect day. They are just surface level things that do not contribute to our essence, nurture our soul, or have anything to do with our well-being. They are not deeply tied to our genius or to our purpose of why we are here. They do not answer the question of "How can I make a contribution to myself, others, or this world?" In this chapter, we want to peel back the layers of a perfect day and help you create one that delivers the things that drive value for your life.

Your Perfect Day

Don't we all just want a bunch of perfect and incredible days? It's amazing what happens when you string a bunch of perfect days together and all of a sudden you start living an amazing life. Can you imagine waking up feeling like every moment was created for you to live, love, give, and play at your best and most joyous self?

So, how do we get to this perfect day? If my perfect day is different from your perfect day, then it stands to reason that designing your perfect day starts with the individual. Time is the great equalizer amongst the human race. It is the one thing that we can't buy or get back, so the faster we realize what makes our days perfect and how to communicate that to everybody around us, the sooner we start living a genius life. This is at the core of Designing Genius, and we start with what a perfect day is to you.

Most people would be stumped if someone asked them, "What is your perfect day?" They may make a joke about needing more sleep or a minute to themselves. But that's a cop-out. That's not a perfect day, that's recovery. Instead, think about it in the smallest details, starting in the morning when you wake up. Before you open your eyes, what do you hear? Are the birds chirping? Are waves crashing on the shore? Does somebody whisper "I love you"? Maybe your kids are giggling? Or your dog is snoring?

Now open your eyes. What do you see? Is there a view of the ocean, mountains, or of a cityscape? What do you see next? Keep scanning the room and your environment until you have a complete picture in your mind of how you would start your perfect day. We want to engage all the senses because it is not just about our external surroundings, but about how it ultimately makes us feel from the inside out. Some people want to feel peace. Some people want to be motivated or invigorated. Others are craving a true sense of belonging, to be connected to their gifts (genius) and know they are contributing that gift to a mission far greater than themselves. It is a very primary need to have relevance in one's life that impacts our sense of value.

At some point, it is time to get out of bed. Are you in a beautiful white nightgown or a big fluffy robe? Is somebody handing you coffee? Maybe you are sitting on the balcony reading the newspaper with your dog snoozing at your feet. Or rushing off to the gym to meet some friends for your favorite exercise class. Continue to think through this perfect day and what comes next. Imagine every moment step by step.

When you can do this minute by minute and be totally aware of what your day feels like then you can call forward and claim these moments as your own. The more clarity you bring to this exercise from beginning to end, the easier it becomes to add more and more of these moments to every day of your life. Think about what happens when you start adding your favorite hobbies, date nights, or a call with a friend to your calendar. Or if you make it a habit to have your favorite flowers in your bedroom. Or technology-free family days on Sunday. Whatever "perfect" means to you is the right definition and is a key part of Designing Genius.

Designing Your Perfect Day

Many of us do not know what our perfect day looks like. We move from one day to the next thinking when we get to a certain point in our life regarding career, money, or age that we will finally get to do the things we enjoy. Most of us are chasing fires and hoping to put them out. Life becomes more like living in a version of *Groundhog Day* until something screams for our attention. Something happens to wake us up from the repetitive patterns that do not serve us. This may be the loss of health, relationships, business opportunities, and maybe most importantly, TIME!

While some put off doing things they enjoy, others do not realize they are already living many of their "perfect day" moments. For example, if your perfect day begins with a loving partner bringing you coffee in bed and someone already does that for you then that moment is already happening. Knowing that a certain percentage of perfect moments are occurring changes the way we think about our life and how we can bring more of those elements into our day. This awareness does two things for us: It provides proof that it is possible to incorporate many perfect day moments every single day, even when we feel life is chaotic and busy. And it makes us grateful for the things that may have gone unappreciated in the past that makes our life enjoyable.

It's never too soon or too early to start creating your perfect day, and it is a great activity to do with your children, life partner, family, friends, and team. Time is so precious. Who wouldn't want to start living their perfect day right now? Think of the impact this can have on a family. If you know what makes up the perfect day for your partner and children, it becomes a guide to help deliver that experience to each other. Suddenly you know what is most important to every member of your household. As your children grow and develop it may become the most significant communication and development tool in your home. It is a way for family members to connect and share affection and respect for each other.

Gift giving becomes much easier. Think about Father's Day, Mother's Day, and birthdays. All you have to do is deliver the perfect day they defined for you. How much easier can it get? And in turn, you will get more from those closest to you too as they execute your perfect day. You will feel seen, heard, valued, and understood because you are getting exactly what you want from the people with whom you want the most connection. And when you feel connected, everything in life is better.

Now it is time to ask yourself, "What is my perfect day?" If you don't know, then who does? A great place to start is to think about your Five Areas of Focus and the Ingredients you chose to go with them. It is important to incorporate those elements into your day if you have identified the elements that will lead to your best and highest self. Starting with "self", ask yourself, "What would I do just for me if my day was absolutely perfect?" To start creating your perfect day, think about your five senses and the what, where, when, why, and how around the following time blocks:

- **Waking Up:** *I wake up in my bedroom overlooking the lake, watching the sunrise. My partner and dog are curled up next to me as I read and drink coffee in bed.*
- **Morning:** *I meditate, stretch, and then hit the gym for my favorite morning workout. Afterward, I eat a healthy breakfast with my family before showering and getting ready for the day.*
- **Work:** *At my home office that overlooks trees and water, I have three priorities to move my business forward, which is to meet with my team to set the vision for a new idea, have a call with a high-profile client, and an interview with a major publication.*

- **Afternoon:** *I meet a friend for a working lunch to discuss new ideas. Afterward, I return emails and read contracts by the pool and then talk to the kids who are returning home from school.*
- **Evening:** *My family plays a game of pick-up basketball and then enjoys an outdoor dinner at an authentic Mexican restaurant. Later that evening, my partner and I spend quality alone time together and prepare for the next day.*

Based on the example above, it is easy to see how this person can start incorporating perfect day moments right now. They may not have the lake house or flexibility to work from home, but they can duplicate the way they wake up and the morning ritual. At work, they can align their business objectives with those of the company and make sure they are prioritizing the most important aspects of their job. Once at home, all the perfect day evening rituals are simple to work into a busy schedule on a regular basis.

What most people don't realize until they complete this exercise is that most of us crave simple but purposeful moments. We are not looking for a string of perfect days with private jets and box office seats. It is not about meaningless encounters with celebrities or lavish events. It's the connection with self and those we love most that come to mind when we start really thinking about what makes up our perfect day.

In our partnership workshops we bring to light a huge misbelief that seems to exist within most relationships. Whether it is a new couple or one that has been together for many years, this misconception versus the reality always surprises people. It is the belief of grand gestures. The mass consumption of social media has created a very unhealthy message that has found its way into many people's beliefs around what is and what is not impressive or worthy. More often than not, when we ask partners what is holding them back from expressing their affection, they tell us that they are waiting to do something grand. Translation: something Instagram or TikTok worthy. My heart sinks every time I hear this.

To quash this notion and quicken the learning on how wrong this thought is, I ask the audience in my workshops to answer one simple question. If you had to choose between one amazing gift, something "wow" like a car, cruise, house, or expensive jewelry, or have frequent small touchstones of "I love you" notes, modest, meaningful gifts, surprise home-cooked meals, or date nights of picnics in the backyard, which would you choose? Almost unanimously, people choose the frequency and the moments of connection. They would rather know who they are to the other person way more often than have the grand gestures that may carry a hefty price tag but carry no meaning. Yet so many people are waiting and straining to pull off some big event.

This is such an aha moment when we realize that our perfect day is attainable and closer than we think in our everyday living. It becomes a matter of pure attraction. We get stronger in self, in our family, partnerships, communities, and purpose. Our genius shows up in it and becomes more clear and more powerful. The clarity around what we want and how to ask for what we want starts to come together when we combine it with our rules of the game.

Imprinting the Perfect Day

Once you design what has meaning to you, it is important to imprint it into your mind using the senses. *Imprinting* is one of the fastest ways to create a new behavior that requires no thinking on your part once it is established. We all have a number of these things that already occur when one of our senses triggers a memory. For example:

- Smelling a certain perfume may remind you of someone you love.
- The sound of church bells may bring memories of the small town you grew up in and the Main Street church you identify with as safe, accepting, loving, and kind.
- Touching a chenille blanket may remind you of hugging your mother in her comfy robe and your childhood. It may be a trigger that immediately softens your soul and energy.
- The scent of lasagna may bring forth memories of Sunday family dinners at your aunt's house. You may feel connected as you remember the loud family chatter in the kitchen.
- Seeing a teeter-totter may remind you of your childhood and playgrounds. This may take you back to a carefree time of laughter on a playground and warm summer days.

As we build our perfect day, we don't just want the tactical things. We want the feelings too. If one of your perfect day moments is to go to your aunt's house for family dinner, then we want to know how that makes you feel. Loved? Connected? Calm? So, now you are working both sides of your brain, both the *being* and *doing* we discussed in Chapter 4.

Now we want to start imprinting that connected and loving feeling we get when we go to our aunt's house for a family dinner. This is where we attach the senses to the experience. What do you smell when you walk in the door? Do you immediately smell lasagna? Or is it a cinnamon scent from a candle burning by the front door? What do you hear? Are your nieces and nephews giggling? A baseball game playing on the television? Walk yourself through the entire experience of when you first walk inside and stand at the threshold. Take in your entire surroundings.

When we do this, we imprint every part of this beautiful experience into our brains. This is why you'll hear someone say,

"Baseball always reminds me of my dad" or "Every time I hear kids giggling it makes me think of my nieces and nephews racing through the house." This does not just trigger the memory, but also the initial feeling associated with it. So, in our previous example of a perfect moment being a family dinner at an aunt's house and how it makes them feel connected and loved, that person can get those same feelings just by smelling lasagna, hearing children giggle, or seeing baseball on television. Those things are attached to them now and forever hold meaning.

It is the same reason why when adults get sick, they crave their mother's chicken noodle soup. It's not just because it makes them feel warm inside, but it is soothing to the soul. They feel nurtured and loved because that's how their mother made them feel when they cared and cooked for them when they were ill.

Imagine imprinting all your favorite things so that you constantly feel nurtured, understood, safe, secure, loved, and peaceful. How amazing would it be to deliver this same experience to your spouse, children, and closest friends? Many people equate the smell of chlorine and Coppertone suntan lotion with the long summer days of their childhood, so just swapping out your current sunscreen for that brand of lotion may remind your spouse of his youth and make him joyful for a day at the pool, splashing with the kids. Even after your kids are grown and out of the house you can still recreate those feelings and emotions between the two of you by sending them reminders or gifts that represent the perfect day moments you shared together.

Perfect Day as an Organization

The educational system has always done a pretty good job of trying to deliver perfect day experiences to their students. Think back to primary school where holidays were celebrated in class with art projects, performances, food, and often celebrations where the parents came in to participate. Even when celebrating Halloween became somewhat controversial, many schools switched over to having a character parade where students dressed as their favorite book character and parents came to watch as they marched around the school.

Colleges have taken it a step further as they now have the responsibility of Thanksgiving, Easter, and other holidays where there are not enough days off from school for most students to go home and spend time with their family. These holidays, which often carry the family tradition of large gatherings, can make a student feel very alone who are stuck at school by themselves. This is why most colleges offer alternatives, gatherings, and support for those left behind.

We can all learn a lot from this practice of understanding what is important to those around us. This allows us to recognize when something is missing and then try to fill that need. Empathy is a word that is front and center in many business and leadership training programs. As people begin the journey of healing from the traumas brought on from COVID, companies and organizations must develop a better understanding and relationship with empathy. Like it or not, people of all ages are healing from a significant number of changes in their life from illness, death, economic issues, childcare concerns, and stress. Those changes are adding adjustments and strain in the workplace. The leaders who learn to address the realities of today's workforce and provide solutions and relief will win. While organizations cannot be expected to address every individual need of a person, there are fundamentals that impact a large majority that can create a tremendous effect on the physical and mental wellness of those around them.

I had a company reach out to me because they were having a difficult time getting their employees to stay focused at work. For many of their employees it was their first professional job. When our Genius trainers did an intake session with the younger people, they discovered what was missing. It was their spring and summer break. They were adults, but their mentality and inner clock was still on those twice a year fun and relaxing breaks. With just a few simple modifications, we suggested the company incorporate some of that nostalgic feeling of spring and summer into the company to bring everyone together.

They hosted a picnic and barbeque lunch with tables outside and encouraged everyone to dress for a hot summer day. They had beach days with music where employees were encouraged to work outside. Just like spring break and summer in college, these events became something the employees looked forward to.

The benefits to the company were even greater than to the employees. Not only did they get energized and focused employees, but something incredible happens when you start moving people around in the business. When you take people from inside the office into the outdoors, change the music, change the food, and bring different people together, it develops new energy. The new energy creates innovation and the stickiness of belonging to the team so that new ideas and relationships grow.

You can't have an experiential office for your clients if you can't create the experience for your own team. So, think about that. When you think about the perfect day, think about how powerful it is as the boss, as the team captain, as the team leader, as the employer, if you knew every single person's perfect day. Think about what would happen if employers started to gift their employees with the things that appeared on their perfect day boards? When you give people the things they wish for, you help them build the life they designed. The loyalty and sense of belonging is stronger than anything gained from a typical training or team-building exercise. Learning to understand an individual's "people language" allows you to have more impact with less energy consistently that gains momentum over time.

> **Dr. Chandra Chela Chomicki's Story**
> Dr. Chandra is a unicorn. She's a bilingual (Spanish/English) African American woman with a PhD and more than twenty-five years of management and leadership experience. She's traveled, lived, and conducted research in over eighty countries.
>
> Her former employer did five reorganizations in a seven-year timeframe. Each time, she was presented with a "new opportunity" to lead the initiative. After she cleaned up one team, another reorg would occur. This led to exhaustion and burnout. With each team she successfully motivated, it became clearer that the central problem of the toxic workplace wasn't the people—it was the executives. So, they parted ways, and she launched her own management consulting company.
>
> She helps leaders struggling with negative and unproductive teams to develop happy productive teams without getting burned out. She offers 1:1 executive coaching, consulting, keynote speaking, and customized leadership training. She is working on bottling her secret sauce into a group coaching program so that she can assist more leaders and offer the support and accountability that other courses do not. She doesn't want to just create another leadership course; she wants to help companies create real sustainable change.
>
> **What did you learn about yourself going through the Designing Genius program?**
> It was very timely for me to go through the course considering this new chapter of full-time entrepreneurship that I am in.

This course helped me identify my One Word, which is "vulnerability". I've always had a job and side businesses, like real estate, but never had to truly be out here on my own.

I finished the Perfect Day activity before, and I have used it even when coaching people. However, I recognize the importance of revisiting my perfect day with some regularity because it had been a while, and my perfect day has changed.

As a wife, mom, and caretaker, I have been more intentional about doing things for myself. I love the fact that you emphasize self-care because even I talk about it, but it can be a struggle to execute. Like so many women, I have competing priorities, and I had to realize that it is not selfish to prioritize myself.

How can Designing Genius help leaders improve their communication and leadership skills?
Like the 5 Love Language books, I believe Designing Genius encourages people to do self-reflection so they can identify what they need to focus on and be able to articulate that to others so that ultimately, they accomplish their highest and best selves. It gives practical activities with examples to help facilitate some of those difficult conversations necessary to propel people further along their personal journeys.

With the new economy (gig, remote workers, etc.) why is personal development so important?
Currently, in the era of employee activism, most employees are on the market. Most employees are free agents and are looking to work for the best and highest bidder. Leaders must learn how to differentiate themselves from other employers by taking the time to figure out what motivates and inspires their staff and what the staff values. As you say, "The inability to align determines

their success." I would add that it determines how *quickly* they will become successful. Unless executive leadership at these companies prioritizes people over profits, they will pay exuberant turnover, training, recruitment, and benefit costs. Their profits will suffer, which is what we are seeing now with so many job openings and some businesses not being able to fully operate because they are understaffed.

It seems like everyone is talking about "well-being" in the workplace. How will leadership need to evolve to address this issue?
I believe there are certain foundational qualities that all leaders must have to effectively persuade a group of people to follow them, but the needs of each team are different. To evolve as a leader, you need to commit to a continual process of listening, learning, executing, evaluating, and innovating. I think that we have two ears and one mouth for a good reason. As leaders, we should listen twice as much as we speak—especially if we hired the right people for the right positions. We need to act upon the best of those ideas, evaluate their performance, then fine tune while always being open to innovative ideas.

Unlocking Tool

Rituals are important for people because they empower us individually or collectively to believe that we can develop, improve, and have some control over a selected outcome. They help us work through difficult problems. They create sticky habits. They encourage us to learn, grow, and connect. Developing a ritual helps you build a new habit and commit to the practice. This is what glues the habit into place, so you are not relying on willpower to carry you through. Willpower is unreliable, but rituals become so ingrained that they become a part of who you are. You see this often in successful people who have strong morning and evening routines. Athletes and performers are the perfect example of people who have a set of rituals and routines they do before and after each event or game to prepare for their performance. These rituals are so ingrained that they can run on autopilot with little thought or motivation.

Create Intentional Rituals
This activity is great for anyone at any stage who wants to create intentional routines and rituals in their lives. Many people wing it during the most critical moments of their day like restful sleep, morning, and evening routines. Systems allow us to experience success on autopilot as our habits and patterns do the heavy lifting. This activity encourages the participant to create the systems they need to be at their highest and best self.

Sleep is essential for health and high productivity, so having a nightly ritual ensures better results. My sleep routine consists of writing, reading, and asking Alexa to play ocean sounds every single evening. If I wake up in the middle of the night, I can repeat my routine to remind my subconscious mind I need to be sleeping. In addition, I have routines for creativity, healing, and health, so when my body experiences these cues it knows what I want it to do.

How to Play
Systems create the process for us to get consistent results. They can be simple like a sleeping routine or more complex like a health and wellness plan. To practice this skill, let's develop a pattern for your bedtime routine and sleep. Consider how to best end your day, wind down, and quiet your mind. Do you like to read? Write? Practice

gratitude or prayer? If there are young kids in the house, then maybe it includes snuggles and storytelling. Regardless of the ritual, the goal is to transition from day and evening to rest. Test out your new ritual and iterate if necessary. This repeatable system is a wonderful process to set up the entire family for peaceful sleep. Here is a template to use for designing a night routine:

- **Three hours before bed:** Stop eating food. There are a number of studies that support your quality of sleep and recovery are much higher when you go to bed with an empty stomach.
- **Two hours before bed:** Stop all blue light electronics. Put away phones and get off social media and stop working and making decisions. You are in an unwinding mode and looking to move the mind, body, and spirit into recovery and rest mode. You can't do this while making decisions.
- **Set your intentions for the next day.** One of my mentors, David Meltzer, helped me get into the practice, or ritual, of starting my next day on the night before. My new day starts at 10 pm, and my first priority is self-care by practicing recovery. This routine allows me to wake up in the morning already in the mindset of pouring into myself, so that I am in a better position to pour into others later.

Chapter 10

Genius Living

We started out this book by asking you, "What if everything you learned about living your best life was wrong?" Not exactly a subtle way to start a book, but when the stakes are as big as living your highest and best life then a little drama is warranted. And since we have already established that we are not living a cartoon fairy tale life where someone else will magically appear to save us, we understand that we are responsible for how we choose to spend the time we have left. This may feel a bit daunting, or not quite how you pictured, but let's think about what a Designing Genius life actually means.

Imagine waking up next to a partner who not only understands and accepts who you are but wants to help you move closer to who you want to be. What would it feel like to be excited and energized at your job? How amazing would it be to give your children the life skills they need to build healthy relationships, find purposeful work, and communicate effectively?

I am a huge fan of professor and author Brené Brown and am continually inspired by her research and work. Her Netflix special, *The Call to Courage* dives into why belonging is so important for business leaders and people to understand. As we continue to think about the places where we spend so much of our precious time, we need to consider what Brown said in her special:

"Vulnerability and belonging is a competitive advantage. Without belonging there is suffering, which leads to all kinds of negative business consequences ... When we build cultures at work where there is zero tolerance for vulnerability, where perfectionism and armor are rewarded and necessary, we can't have productive conversations."

I believe the same is true for any environment where we spend time. Think about what belonging means within schools, communities, families, and people around the world. Everything within Designing Genius is a set of tools that will help you show up as the person you were destined to be. We want you to have the behavior modification tools to release and remove the thoughts and beliefs holding you back from living your perfect day and the life you desire. This book's intention was to help you become fully aware that the only thing standing in your way of the days and life you want... is you!

This is how people get lost. We want and crave what others have without realizing that the cost would be the loss of what we were called to do. We would all be the same person and not the unique individuals we were born to be.

Think of this as players in a game. If we compare players that aren't playing the same game or the same sport, we would get confused. How can you compare yourself to someone who's not playing your position? They don't need your height or skills because the positions are not the same. But there is a skill called your genius that resides inside of you that is absolutely necessary for the position you've been called to play. And if you just simply admire their position without desiring it, you can play your own position and design your own life by celebrating theirs without comparison. If you play your part, then no one can play it like you.

Imagine how powerful it would be to instill this belief system in your children. Instead of wishing and wanting to be like someone they see on social media or at school, they take full ownership of their unique gifts and personality. How it incredible would it be to get them to understand that the further they lean into self, the more sense of belonging they feel from their community and peers? Think of the amazing talents and creativity that would emerge if children felt totally comfortable pursuing the areas of focus that had meaning and joy for them. As parents and educators, we can start helping our children develop this sense of self at any age and stage of their development.

Designing Genius with Children

In our role as parents, we need to connect with the idea that children are growing and developing in phases. This means as they grow from one phase to another, they require different information, energy, and attention from us. As children move from birth all the way through to young adulthood, every stage offers a different layer of social, emotional, and physical growth and development. Each area builds upon the other in its complexities, needs, and milestones. In general, cognitive development means the growth of a child's ability to think and reason. This growth happens differently from ages six to twelve, then from ages twelve to eighteen. Children ages six to twelve years old develop the ability to think in concrete ways. These are called concrete operations.

Once a parent has helped their child learn about concrete thinking and applying logic then they can guide them toward the formal operational stage of thinking. The main difference between the two is that in the concrete operational stage a child is able to think rationally about objects. This means if a child can work with or see the object being discussed then they can make decisions. If they see their teddy bear, they can choose to hug their teddy bear or give it a name.

The formal operational stage is the ability to think rationally without the need to see the object for the thought to be present. They can be lying in bed daydreaming about what to name their teddy bear while their teddy bear is on the floor in another room. This is important for parents to understand when they try and teach kids how to do something that is not a concrete or tangible object in front of them. When parents try to teach kids how to cross a street or spot danger it is nearly impossible in the early years because they do not relate to a conceptual reference like getting hit by a car. The skills required to visualize the danger have not been developed. The parent needs to use other types of teaching to get the desired result since asking them to have the formal thinking is not realistic.

It is important to understand what phase of development your child is in and what that means to you on how you can best meet them and guide their growth. This is critical information when dealing with trauma. For example, with our COVID kids during lockdown they lost almost two years of development as we pulled them out of their learning routines. It is a general guideline to assume that the age of development in which the trauma occurred is often where someone gets stuck mentally in life skills development.

Knowing your child's stage of development allows you to show up with the proper mindset, expectations, and tools to apply your parenting skills in the proper context. For example, when children are young, we tend to speak "at" them. Younger children first learn to do what they are told. As deeper abilities of learning develop, the child begins to question authority. This questioning process is evidence that your child is attempting to learn on a deeper level. Annoying, yes! But needed, as this level of thinking is what allows them to fully develop and practice these deeper thinking skills.

My suggestion to parents is to start the transition of your mindset from being a parent to being a mentor when your child is around the age of twelve to fourteen. This internal shift resets the relationship and begins the transfer of power from being told what to do, to teaching them how to think for themselves.

- What do you think?
- What would you do?
- Why would you do it that way?

I've seen parent and child relationships flourish with this one simple mind shift. You can start implementing Designing Genius with your children and help them harness the tools you are learning here. If they learn and identify how to set their areas of focus, then they will develop the skills to seek and find answers. They will move into protecting their time, boundaries, and relationships by establishing rules that allow them to grow into their highest and best self. These rules will help them build confidence and develop healthy relationships as they mature into adulthood.

Designing Genius for the New Workforce

There has been a huge shift in today's workforce; some believe for the better and others think for the worse. It used to be that a person went out and got a job, moved up the corporate ladder, and retired from that same company with a pension. Whatever needed be done to provide security was the primary objective. How you felt about your job was not a primary driver. Today's workforce is creating their own rules of the game. The Great Resignation is proof that companies need to adjust to attract, retain, and develop their employees' talents in new ways.

The next step a young person takes after high school is not as simple as it once was, where the options were clearly defined. You joined the military, learned a trade, or went on to college. Now, in addition to those opportunities, we have even more. We see kids who graduate high school with prepaid college funds and decide to start a business instead. More options exist for earning professional certifications and licenses that lead to high-paying careers. And then we have the lifestyle entrepreneurs who only need a laptop, access to the Internet, and their skills listed on a couple of freelancer sites who can work from anywhere remotely.

This shift is why it is more important than ever for young people to better understand their identity. Today, people want to live and contribute to the world with more intentionality. With this change in desires and belief systems, the younger generation is on a quest to better understand who they are before choosing an education or career path. When you deepen the understanding of your genius and how the things you enjoy add value in different areas of your life, you begin to see the different career paths available. The modern workforce will experience many different jobs and careers over their lifetime. The huge impact of second and third life careers has reshaped our landscape. When you mix in the rise of the Gig Economy and the Great Resignation, it is abundantly clear that the options for a career today are more customized and flexible than ever before.

No matter what path a student chooses, the first step always needs to start with a deep understanding of their own genius. Once they understand where they are the subject matter expert (SME), the easier it is to determine all the ways they can utilize their genius to earn a living. Having this clarity as to why some activities are energizing to them, while others feel draining, will help them find a career that fills them with excitement and feeds their desire for purpose, meaning, and fulfillment.

And Happily Ever After . . .

And while we've referred to the unrealistic expectations of fairy tales, I think we all aspire to live our highest and best life. Wouldn't it be amazing to sit around a table with your partner, your children, and your friends and share those areas of your life where you are most passionate and energetically focused? Wouldn't it be fun to discover that one of your Ingredients matched that of your son or daughter? Or that your perfect day was just a couple of milestones away from becoming one hundred percent a reality?

What if, moving forward, everything you know about living your best life was actually right?

You have clarity about what areas of your life you want to pour into because the focus is up to you. The ingredients and boundaries are in place to protect those wants and wishes. It is your game and your rules.

That is what it feels like to live a life by design.

Welcome to Designing Genius.

In Gratitude

FROM AMILYA:

May the journey of my own suffering, pain, and healing be transformed into the character that guides my soul. My intention is to transfer my knowledge and heal others from the unintended pain we experience that leads us away from living our very best life.

To David and Lucia:
You are seen, heard, recognized, valued, respected, and so loved. You inspired me to become more and serve greater than I ever thought possible. You are my greatest blessings. Thank you!

For anyone who has ever suffered loss, pain, confusion, or loneliness:

You are wanted and you are welcomed, and I am so glad you are here. This book is for you.

FROM PATRICIA:

Some of us spend our entire lives asking, "Is this as good as it gets?" By having the great honor of knowing and working with so many incredible humans, I have discovered that we all have a beautiful, amazing, and inspiring story that provides the growth that someone else needs.

To my husband Scot:

You are the beginning of my story. My heart started to mend and grow the second I met you. Loving you has always been the easiest thing in my life.

To Max and Jack:

You are both my definition of JOY! Through you, I see, learn, grow, and experience so much. You are always supported, loved, and celebrated for the amazingly unique individuals that you are and will be.

To Amilya:

Your partnership, but mostly your friendship, has given me the next leg of my journey. I am honored to call you my friend and sister.

And to all our friends, family, and supporters:

This book is an expression of gratitude for you. May Designing Genius help you live your highest and best life!

About the Authors

AMILYA ANTONETTI

Amilya Antonetti is one of the most sought-after Human Behavior and Strategic Advisor experts in the world.

She has appeared as a regular business and behavior expert on *The Oprah Winfrey Show*, *The Steve Harvey Show*, and *Dr. Phil*. She has built or advised on over two billion in sales for companies and high-profile clients such as Steve Harvey, Mike Tyson, Listerine Strips, Sharper Image, Cold Stone Creamery, George Foreman, and more.

Her "in the trenches" experience developing people, deep knowledge in building the value drives in a business, and her Designing Genius systems, programs, and "behavioral toolbox" makes her a leading expert on "people problems" that have grown during our Great Resignation and rise of the remote worker. Combining this know-how with her work ethic and her incredible ability to immediately impact one's mindset and NEXT RIGHT action steps makes her an invaluable asset to those who want to succeed in today's fast, competitive, and "people first" landscape.

Amilya's vision for a healthier relationship between people and companies has earned her global respect and numerous awards, including:

- The Women's Economic Forum – "Women of the Decade 2019 Award"
- Wells Fargo – "Fastest Under Forty"
- "Best Places to Work" (three-time winner)

- The Kauffman Foundation – Entrepreneur Award
- She has grown seven clients onto Inc.'s 500 list
- She has been nominated twice to Ernst & Young's "Entrepreneur of The Year"
- She has been featured in *People, Time, Forbes, Inc., Smart Money,* and *Entrepreneur,* and has been named in "The 55 People You Must Meet" by Jack Canfield.

Today, Amilya is the CEO and Creator of Designing Genius, a powerful training and licensing platform that changes the paradigm on how companies, opportunities, and our greatest asset "THE PEOPLE" come together as we answer the call of the Gig Economy.

PATRICIA WOOSTER

Patricia is a former software executive-turned-founder of WoosterMedia Publishing, where they help experts, leaders, executives, and entrepreneurs convert their intellectual property into print and digital products so they can build brand awareness and reach a global audience. Her clients include C-Level executives, college professors, professional athletes, and media personalities. They have landed agents, major publishing contracts, speaking opportunities, and bestseller status.

She is the author of eighteen books, including the award-winning and bestselling book *Ignite Your Spark* with Simon & Schuster.

Patricia helps her clients amplify their message and leverage their expertise into books, digital courses, workshops, speeches, consulting, and media opportunities. Her experience ranges from working with companies and organizations like Disney, Home Shopping Network, WeDay, Informix Software, and KPMG to working with start-up entrepreneurs and influencers.

Today, Patricia is the CIO of Designing Genius, a powerful training and licensing platform that changes the paradigm of how companies and people reach their highest and greatest potential. She directs the in-house development of Designing Genius products and services while assisting clients, consultants, and companies in the development of their people through the use of products, services, and tools to solve "people problems" through transformational behavior modification techniques.

Visit www.DesigningGenius.com

Additional Free Bonus

Jumpstart Your Designing Genius Journey!

If you are ready to start designing your genius life and want to create your blueprint, take the first step by enrolling in our Designing Genius course where we will walk you through the process from start to finish. In one weekend, you will have your entire journey mapped out with the action steps necessary to achieve your vision and dreams. Scan the QR code below for more details.

- Create your blueprint for Designing Genius in your life
- Set your Should and Should Not's for genius living
- Put actions behind where you are now to where you want to be
- Design and live your Perfect Day over and over again
- Use the Coupon Code "BONUS" for $50 off the course

Start Designing Genius today.

Thank You

Thank You For Reading our Book!

We really appreciate all of your feedback, and we love hearing what you have to say.

We need your input to make the next version of this book and our future books even better.

Please leave us a helpful review on Amazon letting us know what you thought of the book.

Thank you so much!

Amilya Antonetti & Patricia Wooster

www.ingramcontent.com/pod-product-compliance
Lightning Source LLC
LaVergne TN
LVHW041334080426
835512LV00006B/453